What Readers Are Saying

I loved the book... As my wife and I read, we could see how the principles in the book not only applied to the business world but to our family as well.

Joey Burns, Real Estate Businessman,
Father of Five, Colorado

Clear and compelling—a good blend of principles and personal story.

Brett Johnson,
Business Consultant & Author,
Father of Three, California

A quick read. Well written and very applicable to a number of issues I am currently wrestling with.

Richard Rock, Wealth Manager,
Father of Two, California

I was hooked... Very, very powerful. I look forward to taking friends and even our pastor through it.

Justin Forman,
Executive Vice President of
Publishing Company, Father of One, Texas

This is a very good book, one that seems to be a natural follow-on to "God is at Work." ... Ken's new book helps us see how to live out our faith in our daily work lives, and impact our co-workers, even our surrounding neighborhoods and culture. As it turns out, in my own journey of faith, I am, right now, asking some of the same questions Ken addresses. This is a timely book for me.

Rick Thrasher,
Computer Software Professional,
Father of Three, California

Truly like intellectual and spiritual manna! Very timely in my life ... Real business wisdom coming from someone who has been there—and has successfully done that.

Brad Zielinski,
Sales Manager, Single, California

Really enjoying the book. I'm hooked.

Mark Bucko, Pastor,
Father of Three, California

Relevant and well written ... speaks directly to many of the issues of misunderstanding experienced by Christian business leaders.

Duane Moyer, Marketing Director,
Father of Three, Georgia

Praise for The Integrated Life

Ken Eldred writes compellingly about the "Sunday-Monday Gap," sharing real-life examples of how this split impoverishes both our faith life and our busi.ness life. Eldred takes us out of this false choice, and offers wonderful wisdom and stories about how to live an integrated and abundant life.

Professor David W. Miller, Director,
Princeton University
Faith & Work Initiative

For years I have been blessed and challenged by the life and ministry of Ken Eldred. My prayer is that this book will challenge many to live out their faith in the high-pressure world of business, technology, and finance in the same real, vibrant, and pervasive way.

Dr. Luis Palau, World Evangelist

Ken Eldred has addressed a topic that has confused and bewildered Christians for years—how to reconcile your faith and your work. Whether you are a CEO or a bagboy at the supermarket, this book will show you how you can transform people, organizations and communities by serving others to glorify God.

Dr. John E. Mulford, Former Dean of
Graduate School of Business, Regent University

Dr. Eldred's unique added distinctive is his skill to translate spiritual values into the business equation where it connects and convinces the most astute MBA. Never have I heard a man who speaks with greater effect upon an audience! ... a must read, chock full of the nuggets of wisdom that have made Dr. Eldred such a rare find!

Dr. Jerry Johnston, Senior Pastor,
First Family Church, Kansas City, Kansas

I have been privileged to work with Ken Eldred for 40 years and watch him truly integrate his faith and business skills to build profitable businesses and impact lives in the marketplace. This book can be instrumental in helping believers to integrate their faith and their work to be personally fulfilled and more successful as they work to transform the marketplace and society.

John B. Mumford, Founding Partner,
Crosspoint Venture Partners

Ken Eldred has proven his extraordinary gifts in the areas of faith and business over the years, and now he has been proficient in connecting these two crucial elements of success seamlessly in his latest book ... I highly recommend that you read and study Ken Eldred's latest book which is tremendous in its scope and vision.

Dr. Yonggi Cho, Founding Pastor,
Yoido Full Gospel Church, Seoul, Korea

THE INTEGRATED LIFE

EXPERIENCE THE POWERFUL ADVANTAGE
OF INTEGRATING YOUR FAITH AND WORK

Copyright © 2007-2010

Published by Manna Ventures, LLC
Montrose, Colorado, U.S.A.
Printed in the U.S.A.

ISBN: 978-0-9840911-1-9

1 2 3 4 5 6 7 8 9 10 / 15 14 13 12 11 10

Rights for publishing this book in other formats or languages are contracted by Manna Ventures, LLC.

For additional information, visit mannaventures.org

Cover Photo © Glenn Jenkinson — fotolia.com

Table of Contents

Dedication

To my grandchildren, Nathaniel, Daniel, Addy, David, Ariel, Deborah, Gwendolyn, and those to come—and to yours. I pray they, like their parents, will carry the torch of faith, the light of Christ into every aspect of their lives. May the Lord give them a double portion of wisdom to exceed the knowledge they will possess in the years to come and lead them to understand, inspire, and impact the world for him.

Foreword

I find that believers generally understand how their faith relates to their church work, spiritual life, and perhaps even family life. But many are unable to find a meaningful connection between their spiritual life and their work life. As a result, they live in a fragmented way and miss out on the abundant life at work. That's why this book needed to be written. It's a paradigm-changer with transformational implications for your life.

As Ken Eldred unfolds things, the church abounds with Christians who adopt their work principles and objectives from the prevailing business culture. Believers all too rarely recognize spiritual value in everyday business—let alone have any way to view and perform work as an act of worship. Consequently, many followers of Jesus tend to see their jobs as lacking redeeming value. They separate work and worship/ministry into different compartments and become spiritually drained rather than healthily fulfilled with a joyous sense of God's pleasure and purpose in their work.

This book gives you the why and the how for living an integrated life in which your faith gives purpose to your work. Ken Eldred reveals how your daily work in the business world can be an act of worship, a ministry of serving others to the glory of God. Your job in whatever vocation you serve is as "spiritual" in its potential meaning as my role as a pastor-shepherd. In God's eyes, your work and mine is worship and ministry as we serve others to the glory of God, whether in the church or in the marketplace. It isn't about what we do but about who we are in Christ, why we do our jobs, and how we approach life.

Ken Eldred has hit at the heart of the matter, showing us how a large portion of our life, our work life, can be redeemed. He approaches this subject from the perspective of a seasoned businessman. He's not a theologian, but I think that only enhances the power of his writing and the pertinence of his examples. Having lived his life in the business world, Ken is dynamically gifted to help fellow "laymen" capture spiritual reality in the most pragmatic terms—in ways you'll be enriched to discover. His message is one we all need to hear, understand, and apply.

If you're one of Ken's fellow believers in the marketplace, I encourage you to discover how your faith and your work—and indeed, your whole life—can be more deeply integrated. I encourage you to join with a couple of friends to work through these ideas together. Study and debate them. I pray the Holy Spirit will lead you as you read this book and are encouraged that God has a deep interest in your work life. And if you're a pastor, may you enjoy Jesus' expanded vision for His church. Let's take up the calling to equip followers of Jesus for ministry at work. I guarantee this book will help many people for whom an integrated, abundant life remains elusive.

Jack W. Hayford
Founding Pastor, *The Church On The Way*
Chancellor, *The King's Seminary and College*

PART I

The Way Things Are

In the back of our minds there's a plaguing sense that something is unresolved. We're trying to keep our heads above water, but there never seems to be enough time for it all. We're working so hard just to keep up. Many of us sense that our professional lives and our personal lives are at odds. We may even feel that our work and our faith are pulling us in opposite directions.

Throughout my journey, I have encountered various questions about the relationship between my faith and my work. I'm sure you've asked yourself a number of these profound questions as well. (Chapter 1) Why does it seem more difficult than ever to align our faith and our work? (Chapter 2) And what have we done to cope with the deep disconnect in our lives? (Chapter 3) Let's take a quick look at the way things are—and what got us to this state.

Unanswered Questions

What's Faith Got to Do With It? (Part I)

"Hey, Rich, take a look at this!" Incredulous, I had already read it several times. First I was shocked, now I was reduced to laughter. Could this be for real? I summoned the leader of my team to check it out.

"Let me see that," said Rich, a young, bright Harvard Business School graduate several years my senior. He headed up the acquisitions group for a part of American Standard, a Fortune 500 conglomerate in New York City with interests in many areas of business. Armed with undergraduate and MBA degrees from Stanford, I had joined American Standard in part because of the toughness I perceived in New York business people. I could use some toughening up, I thought. Rich's reaction was more serious than mine; this was definitely not a laughing matter. "Uh, oh," we both thought.

American Standard was considering the purchase of a Midwest manufacturing firm, and we were reviewing the business. In evaluating this potential acquisition, my role was to thoroughly analyze its business plan, market, and market position, while others reviewed the financials of the company. It was pretty heady stuff for a young guy fresh out of business school. This Midwest company was small compared to American Standard, but it had a strategic position in the market. It was very strong in construction products and boasted a favorable sales growth and earnings record. From the financial records, the company appeared to be run very well. From a marketing point of view, it seemed to be on target for continued success.

During my visit to the company's headquarters, I went to the president's office and requested a copy of the five-year strategic plan. Sitting down in my makeshift office, I cracked it open and began to read. Like most plans, it started with the company's objectives, scope of the business, competition, and so forth. These statements normally address financial goals, position in the market, vision, and objectives—what the company wants to be and what the thrust of its business will be. I was there to learn and look for any management weaknesses in the company, within the marketing effort or elsewhere. So the first thing I focused on was the objectives statement. It's the most important statement in the document; you can tell a lot about management from what it does and does not say.

There it was, a simple single sentence fragment: "To glorify God in all that we do." What!? I was taken aback. How could any reasonable business executive team write an objective like that? Expecting something I could evaluate using analytical methods I'd learned in business school, instead I got some theological statement!

They'd switched categories on me. Were these guys running a church or a company? I wasn't a "church type." But even if I was, I saw no place for God at work.

Rich and I didn't even know where to start with their objectives statement. I moved on to review the rest of the document, which seemed pretty solid. But I remained concerned about what I had read at the outset. If that business objectives statement was the best they could do, I concluded, this company's management team must be pretty weak. Rich was downright concerned. Management was planning to keep the present executive team in place after the acquisition, and now it was unclear to him whether they'd be capable of running the business going forward. As business strategists, we continued our review of the company. Unable to analyze or comprehend the company's religious objective statement, we dismissed it as some sort of aberration not worth further thought. We found the business sound and made an offer. The purchase of the company was soon completed, and its products were subsumed into the American Standard mix of products.

Reinforced by my prestigious business school education, I saw no role for the spiritual life in the marketplace. Business is business. What's faith got to do with it? Faith belongs in a whole different compartment, I thought.

What's the Goal?

Two years later, I found myself the strategic planning manager for American Standard's U.S. plumbing and heating division. I was an individual contributor, a one-man band except for some secretarial support. One day, the head of the division called me into his office, and in the next half hour changed my life forever. "Ken, I've decided to promote you," he said. He outlined my new responsibilities, and I walked out of his office suddenly in charge of 350 people in seven groups with an office and salary to match. At age 27, I was over the moon. What an incredible opportunity and experience! I went home after work so energized I could think of nothing else.

That night in bed I began to contemplate my future. I lay there for hours working through all the places this career move could take me. In my mind, I had it all—wealth, position, and fame—it would just be a matter of time. Then in the darkness, when I was spent in my reverie, a troubling question formed in my mind, seemingly from nowhere. A very sick and nauseated feeling swept over me as I lay there in my dark room, contemplating the emptiness of those plans I had laid out for my life. *Is this all there is? It all seems so pointless*, I thought. *What if I wake up some day at age 60 and discover that I have missed* it—*and I don't even know what* it *is!* It was a haunting and sobering thought. Were the objectives I was pursuing in the business world—profit, wealth, position, fame—really what it's all about?

At some time or another, the notion that we may be chasing the wrong goal must enter the mind of everyone engaged in the economic enterprise. But we usually try to ignore it, because it seems like an impossible problem to solve. I certainly didn't have a satisfying answer. So I plunged into my new work, and for a while, I managed to put those troubling ideas out of my mind. I could see clear skies, upward mobility, and a trajectory of success.

But soon my world came crashing down. I was hit with seven of the top ten stress producers all at once. My father passed away suddenly without warning. He was the man I respected and loved the most. My young marriage was in desperate need of repairs. So was the house we'd just bought. My boss was replaced, and my job was changed. We weren't doing well as a division, and with the arrival of a new management team I perceived my new position as a demotion. My new team was smaller, riddled with serious problems, and saddled with profit-and-loss responsibility. To make matters worse, my new group was losing money. Then we found out my wife Roberta had what appeared to be a serious health problem.

Over the next two years, I struggled with these issues. While I had major successes with my new business role, nothing seemed to get better in the other areas of my life. I just wanted to get rid of all my problems and felt a move back to California would be the solution. So I quit my job, my wife quit hers, and we crossed the country with a U-Haul trailer in tow. We found an apartment and settled in. It was great to be home. I set out to find a job. We felt better, and it seemed like we were on a path to correcting our problems. On the surface that may have been the case, but nothing was really settled in our lives. Something was still missing at the core.

What's Faith Got to Do With It? (Part II)

Roberta and I resolved to give our young son Eric a chance to decide about religion. It was an opportunity we'd both been given in our early years, and we wanted to afford him the same. In good executive fashion, I put together a plan for us to follow. We would start out by attending the church I grew up in, a Presbyterian church, then we'd try the church Roberta grew up in, a Catholic church. Then why stop there? We would sample the Buddhist temple, the local synagogue, and whatever other religious traditions we could find.

As we walked into the church the first Sunday morning, the warmth we experienced surprised us. It was a personal sensation hard to describe, but we both felt it. We stayed. Roberta joined a women's group, and I joined the men's group to learn more. No commitment, we were just checking it out.

Soon, I ventured into reading the Bible. I wasn't expecting it to hold up to scrutiny or to relate to modern-day realities, but I was actually surprised on both accounts. Not long after that, I began talking to God. I was learning but also struggling to get a handle on what the implications were for my life.

One Sunday morning, the sermon really tugged on me to make a decision about who was the God of my life. The struggle was simply this: *If I agree to accept you as Lord and Savior*, I thought, *then I will have to become a missionary in some far-off land or a pastor in the poor section of our town.* I wasn't opposed to the ministry per se, but it would mean abandoning the passion I had for business. I had a great background for business and almost five years of experience. I felt I could be good at it and really wanted a chance.

But I thought a career in business simply wouldn't be good enough if I were required to be fully committed to God, to make him first in everything. If I wanted to pursue spiritual objectives and serve him, I'd have to go into the ministry. How could I truly please God in the corporate world? What does that environment have to do with the things that matter to God? Lacking any examples to the contrary, I saw no role for the truly spiritual in the marketplace. Businessmen and -women are not serious about their faith, I concluded. Those really committed to God serve him, and the place to do that is in the ministry. Ministry is ministry. Business is business.

Business or Ministry?

The job search was going slowly, and my time and financial resources were running out. As I stood in the parking lot that Sunday after church, I knew that Jesus was Lord and that I needed to accept him regardless of where that thread would lead. I surrendered to him my career and my plans. I submitted to his authority and waited to see what would happen next.

Business or ministry—which would it be? While seeking guidance, I discovered Psalm 37:4, which says: "Delight yourself in the Lord and he will give you the desires of your heart." My desire was for business, but was that a biblical desire? Was that something God would give? I prayed that God would change my desire for business if his plan for me really was in the ministry. But if he was willing to give me the desire of my heart for business, I prayed, then he would need to open my eyes to the business opportunities around me.

Does God Care About Business?

God answered my prayers by providing a job. A small company with a new product needed a head of marketing. It wasn't just any job but one that really fit what I needed most. I found myself identifying with the experience of Abraham, whom God had asked to offer his only child Isaac (Gen. 22:1–18). My "child" was my career in business. Like Abraham, I wasn't ultimately required to go through with the sacrifice. God was more interested in the demonstration of my willingness. And now he was granting me the desires of my heart!

When I joined the company, I wasn't sure how I'd perform in the role. At American Standard, my confidence had been in my own skill sets and abilities. But now I wouldn't have the support that's normally available in a large organization. We couldn't afford the normal information sources or additional consulting help. How was I to function in that situation? On whom or what could I rely? And how did my new relationship with God fit in with all of this?

I had this notion that weakness drove people to call out to God, and I certainly didn't consider a lack of strength a virtue. But I also realized I couldn't do it alone. The psalmist writes, "I lift up my eyes to the hills—where does my help come from? My help comes from the Lord, the Maker of heaven and earth" (Ps. 121:1–2). Could that apply to my business? Does God really care about what happens in the marketplace? I wasn't sure, but I needed help. This was all new to me.

How Do You Include God In Your Business?

I found myself wishing my earthly father were around to help me. He'd been a successful businessman, starting from nothing to running the Hewlett-Packard Company before his untimely death. I longed for a mentor in my father, but of course that wasn't possible.

Perhaps I could partner with God? Sure would be nice to partner with him, I concluded in my young Christian life. Here was a potential partner who had greater wisdom, knowledge, and capability than I would ever possess. Not only that, but he was now my father! Surely he'd want to help me wherever I needed it. *But how does one bring him into the equation? Will God really do the miraculous to help me in business? And isn't asking him to bless my work a selfish request?* I would wrestle with these questions, as I sought to determine what role God should have in my work.

In due course, the company I'd joined was sold. It was time to move on. I felt God's urge to start a business. One day, I was vetting some business ideas with a friend. He listed a number of thoughts, and at one point I distinctly heard a voice in my head. In fact, it was the same voice I'd heard years ago asking, "Is that all there is?" This time, the voice said, "**That's it.**" As my friend continued listing ideas for businesses, I responded in my mind, "What's it?" The answer was, "The company you should start." I asked my friend and future partner to cycle back through the ideas until he came to the one God had spoken to me about. "Let's pursue that venture," I concluded.

Together we founded Inmac, a company that sold computer accessories by mail order to minicomputer users. It was the mid-1970s; only businesses owned computers. They were called minicomputers, though we would certainly not use that term today to describe these hunks of metal. But in an age where a computer could occupy an entire room, these qualified as "minicomputers."

I began the company and my workday with prayer. I still wasn't exactly sure what it meant, but I was determined to have God be a partner in my business. Early on, I invited my pastor to come and visit Inmac, thinking he'd have some answers. He was a wonderful man of God, but after looking at all that we were doing, he finally admitted he had no clue how to help me. I invited another pastor who was known to be interested in business to come and share with me. We had a lengthy meeting in which he gave me some insights, but ultimately it left me with little to go on.

I sought ways to bring God into the business in every way beyond my prayer life. I really had no idea what to do. I fumbled around in the dark, but I kept experiencing miracles that continued to spur me on. You'll find many of them recounted throughout this book.

Questions of the Journey

Over the years, Inmac went through ups and downs. But God was good. What started out as a two-person venture with $5,000 and a grocery bag of computer connector parts grew to a company of 1,500 employees in ten countries with $400 million in annual sales. Along the way, in 1986, Inmac had an IPO. Almost ten years later, we sold the company to Micro Warehouse, and I exited the business.

An idea God gave me became the basis for another startup company called Ariba. My long-time friend John Mumford, a Christian brother who is the founding director of Crosspoint Venture Partners, helped develop and mold the business concept. Our idea was to use the emerging Internet to simplify the inefficient, complex way companies purchase from suppliers. The founding team included some colleagues who'd been at Inmac as well as some from Benchmark Capital Partners. Ariba was founded in 1996. Three years later, Internet companies were hot and the few business-to-business Internet companies like Ariba were even hotter. It was the darling of Wall Street and went public with a market value of $6 billion. During the next year, Ariba would be worth as much as $40 billion!

Over the course of my years in business, there were a number of questions I was forced to ask about faith and work. Is work in the ministry really a higher calling? Is it my calling? Does God care about business? What is the goal of business? Is there a connection between faith and business? Spiritual life and business life seem to operate in different spheres that have little intersection; is there a way to integrate my faith and my work? If so, what is the role of faith in business? When do I apply my talent and training, and when do I leave things to God? And how do I partner with God in my business?

Perhaps you're asking some of these same questions today. If so, this book is for you. You may be finding, as I did, that the approaches and goals you learned in your formal or informal business training leave you with unanswered questions about the role of your faith. Like me, you may also be finding little support in the church. Some fellow believers in business have adopted methods and objectives in the marketplace that don't reflect their faith. Pastors typically don't discuss business issues from the pulpit or validate everyday work as a ministry and a calling. And chances are you don't know of a church program devoted to equipping people for ministry in their work lives.

The challenge is to integrate the ageless and immutable truths of God with our work in the marketplace. But unfortunately, that's becoming a growing challenge. Connecting our daily work with biblical values and the example of Jesus isn't getting any easier. Here's why.

CHAPTER 2

Trying to Keep Up

I think there is a world market for maybe five computers.
(IBM Chairman Thomas Watson, 1943)

Outsourcing is nothing less than a full-fledged mega-trend both here in the U.S. and around the world.
(Fortune Magazine, 1995)

There are never enough hours in a day, but always too many days before Saturday.
(Hanson's Treatment of Time)

The Good Ol' Days

My father worked with Bill Hewlett and Dave Packard from the early days of their startup venture. Not only has HP become one of the largest, most successful computer companies of all time, but it's spawned many other innovative technology firms. So I've witnessed the Silicon Valley high tech industry grow from a single sapling to a forest.

I occasionally encounter elderly folks, including family members, who have lived here all their lives and remember the days when there were no technology companies in the area. They wax nostalgic at their childhood. Life was simple, the valley was filled with orchards and ranches, towns were identified by large open country in between, traffic wasn't a problem, technology was simple, and real estate was inexpensive. They barely recognize today's Silicon Valley filled with office complexes, urban sprawl, technological breakthroughs, bumper-to-bumper traffic, and young knowledge workers who could become overnight billionaires. Ah, the good ol' days.

The Only Constant Is Change

Today we're in a brave new world. Business is tough and increasingly global and competitive. The marketplace and individual jobs are undergoing dramatic shifts, often in response to groundbreaking advances in technology. Both the volume and availability of information are constantly increasing. If you suspect things are moving faster today than ever, you're right, and the implications for us are staggering.

Faster and Faster

In the 1960s, Intel co-founder Gordon Moore observed that the computing power available for a given price was doubling every two years. He predicted that this trend would continue into the future, and it has. This may not seem significant, but consider that something that continues to double every set period of time isn't just undergoing linear growth—it's actually growing exponentially!

This exponential growth has held up for at least a century, and there's evidence to suggest it will continue.[1] If Moore's Law continues to hold, the computational power of one human brain (2×10^{16} calculations per second) will cost

$1,000 by 2023. By 2037, it will cost one cent![2] Technological advances will affect our jobs, companies, industries, and required skills, but the accelerating rate of change makes it very difficult to envision the future. And that uncertainty leaves us anxious or even fearful.

The Insecurity of Jobs

When you order from the drive-thru at the McDonald's off U.S. interstate highway 55 near Cape Girardeau, Missouri, you'll get fast, accurate, and pleasant service. But if you'd expect to see the face behind the friendly voice at the pickup window, you'd be mistaken. Little do you know that the person taking your order is at a call center more than 900 miles away in Colorado Springs, Colorado. The call center workers earn slightly more than restaurant employees, but by cutting order time by about a third and mistakes by a half, they're said to be well worth the extra pay.[3] *How soon until fast food jobs are outsourced to India?* you might be asking. *And if minimum-wage jobs aren't safe, is mine?* It's a question many of us in the marketplace think about.

Outsourcing and offshoring have evoked fear and anxiety in many of us working in the Western world. "The truth is that we are living through a moment of maximum uncertainty," says BusinessWeek. "Outsourcing looms large as a potential threat because no one knows how many jobs and which industries are vulnerable."[4] Globalization is putting everyone in the game and allowing the rest of the world to catch up. And we're feeling the heat.

Not only are many jobs moving to lower-cost locations; some are disappearing altogether. Consider telephone operators, who were once the backbone of the telephone industry. Today their functions are almost entirely automated. Secretaries are a thing of the past. Dictation and letter writing have given way to the Internet and handheld communication devices. In every industry we see jobs changing or disappearing.

Those jobs that aren't moving or disappearing are undergoing rapid change. All of us are impacted by technology in one way or another. No one is immune. Whatever happens in the future, we know that the work we do now will change materially.

The Insecurity of Companies

Nothing makes us more uncomfortable than the growing "topple rate," the rate at which top companies lose their positions as market leaders. A McKinsey study looked at companies in the top 20 percent in revenue in their industries and monitored how many dropped out of that leadership group within five years. It found that between 1975 and 1995 the topple rate for these firms doubled. The authors also suggested that it could double again in the next two decades.[5]

Who would have imagined that industry leaders like General Motors would fall so quickly? GM led global auto sales for 77 straight years, from 1931 to 2007.[6] Less than two years later, the company filed for Chapter 11 bankruptcy protection and only survived due to a bailout by the United States government. There is less and less security in being large and established.

The Insecurity of Industries

I've seen entire industries come and go in what seems like a flash. Consider the minicomputer, which predated the PC. You may not have heard of it, but Digital Equipment Corporation (DEC) was a pioneer in the American computing industry. During the 1970s and '80s, its PDP and VAX minicomputers were arguably the most popular with the scientific and engineering communities. At its peak in the late 1980s,

DEC employed more than 100,000 people. It was the second-largest computer company in the world.

But microcomputers soon entered the scene, and DEC never recovered. Its proprietary technology quickly lost out to smaller machines with more open architectures. Layoffs followed layoffs, and divisions were sold off. Within ten years of its height, DEC was no more. The entire minicomputer industry went from cradle to dominance to grave in two short decades.

Today, the life cycle of industries and corporations can run even shorter. Virtually everyone is vulnerable. We're left with a sense that there's no security in the marketplace. Jobs aren't safe; companies aren't safe; industries aren't safe.

What will the world and the marketplace look like in the future? Will my skills still be in demand? Change, especially change we can't really envision, evokes a sense of uncertainty and fear. And that insecurity places a huge burden on us.

The Unsettled Free Agent

While past generations were content to spend decades at a large company working toward a pension, today's marketplace is filled with free-agent workers who have little attachment. Anxious workers no longer entrust themselves to corporations, let alone to a single company. Our security is in our degrees, experience, and skill sets rather than in the established, secure corporate name of our employer. We bounce around from organization to organization, chasing greater salaries, responsibilities, or personal fulfillment. The question often asked is "How can I profit from this opportunity?" Commitment is viewed as an outdated impediment to realizing our potential.

Today it's everyone for himself. People now operate from their own agendas, and the mantras in the workplace have become "Watch out for number one" and "Cover your back-side." The resulting environment is an individualistic, macho jungle with a "gotcha" attitude. In this godless climate we're left to question whether God has any role in business at all.

One of the reasons workers are often transient free agents these days is that they're constantly seeking meaning, fulfillment, and happiness in their jobs. But in many cases that goal remains elusive. They seek fulfillment in terms of material rewards and personal prestige and then bemoan the fact that they find no pleasure in the everyday tasks they perform. People are actually less fulfilled and more likely to experience meaninglessness in their lives and work than ever before.[7]

The level of dissatisfaction experienced at work leads many to adopt a very negative attitude toward their daily occupation. We're just getting through it, doing our time, constantly looking over our shoulders or considering other work options. Work is seen as a cost, the price one must pay. Already resigned to a miserable work experience, we look to hobbies, entertainment, travel, and ministry for joy and personal fulfillment.

No Time to Think

Technological improvements can increase our productivity and effective wages and suppress the cost of goods we buy. But these advances carry a cost. We have so much change and information to process just to stay abreast of all the developments related to our jobs, companies, competitors, industries, and technologies. Information is so readily available, and the rate of progress is so fast. It can be overwhelming just trying to keep up with it all! But if we're going to be effective in our work, we need to invest the time and energy it takes to stay on the cutting edge.

On top of the demands from our work, we need to honor other commitments in our lives. Often these various obligations conflict or collide, and something has to give. Outside obligations seem to infringe on our ability to succeed at home, and serving God is one more thing for which we don't seem to have the bandwidth. We feel we simply don't have enough hours to excel in all areas of our lives. Many of us are left overextended and pulled in different directions.

Unfortunately, we also lack the resources to tackle the additional challenge of connecting our faith with our work. We simply don't have the time to process what's happening. We're near or at a moment where the speed of life and technology are leaving us behind, as we run to catch this parting train. There is simply little time to reflect—let alone do more.

And even if we did have the capacity, the task of bringing the immutable truths of God to bear on our constantly changing workplace is like trying to hit a target that's moving rapidly in unpredictable directions. So as our lives take a pounding from workplace influences, we're left with an unsettling sense of disconnectedness.

We Are Led to Conclude

There are some profound forces that are heightening the tension at work—and thus the tension between work and faith—for many in the business world. Technology is advancing at an ever-increasing rate. Competition is intensifying across borders; we're now facing a world economy. An ever-increasing amount of information must be digested just to keep up. Performance demands on the worker are as high as ever, even as we sense that our jobs, companies, and industries are less stable and secure. The relationship between companies and employees is changing; there's less commitment between individuals and organizations. All these forces affect the way we look at work, perform our work, commit to work, value our work, and enjoy our work.

Challenged with the fast-paced, turbulent work environment and competing commitments to family and faith, we rarely find the time or resources to resolve the host of unsettling and unsatisfying feelings that believers in the business world may experience. We may find ourselves identifying with some of these:

- I can't seem to balance the demands of work, family, and spiritual life. The competitive forces and personal demands of the workplace leave me with the sense that there's an irresolvable tension between succeeding at work and succeeding at home.
- I feel so insignificant in the scheme of things. In reality I'm just getting by at work. Or in reality I have triumphed only through sheer luck. Either way, I don't want to tell anyone.
- I can't seem to reconcile my work with a desire to serve God. I feel the need to leave the business world in order to really please him.
- I don't really subscribe to the materialistic objectives of business. Making a profit off someone else just doesn't seem noble.
- I really ought to be doing something else—if only I could. The dog-eat-dog world of business is no place for a serious Christian.
- I am preoccupied with so many issues that at any time could affect my job, leaving little time to consider the relation between my work and God.

The current marketplace is a fast-paced jungle, and many of us feel ill equipped to navigate it. We're finding it difficult or impossible to reconcile the increasing demands of the marketplace with those of our home and spiritual lives. Family, church, work—they all want and deserve a piece of our time. They all demand our focus, commitment, and investment. How do believers cope with these competing interests? How does anyone survive in this competitive and unreliable work environment and yet maintain a vibrant personal faith?

One Christian author suggests that when you return home from work, you leave all your workday problems outside the front door. You should imagine your work issues and concerns being like a coat you take off and hang on a tree. When you leave for work the next morning, you simply pick them up again as you walk out the door. This might sound like sage advice, but it leaves us with a life of different worlds, values, and rules that do not intersect. When putting on our work coats in the morning, many of us will leave behind our family and faith coats. I've come to realize that this is a coping mechanism that's part of the problem rather than part of the solution. It's called compartmentalization, and many of us reflect it without even realizing it.

CHAPTER 3

The Compartmentalized Life

Religion has become privately meaningful and publicly irrelevant.

(Dr. Peter L. Berger, Boston University)

Integrity means my whole life is integrated together—no secular, no spiritual.

(Rick Warren, author, pastor)

The harmony of [God's] being is the result not of a perfect balance of his parts, but of the absence of parts ... He does not divide himself to perform a work, but works in the total unity of his being.

(A. W. Tozer, author, pastor)

Our Coping Mechanism

In order to cope with the demands of work, family, and faith, we have created a solution, the compartmentalized life. We operate in more or less segmented spheres that have little overlap. I cannot give you all the research to support this conclusion except to say that I see it everywhere. And I myself bought into the concept early in my walk with Christ.

What are the compartments we live in? Here are some of the most prevalent.

The *family life* compartment includes our spouse, children, extended family, and close friends—and how we deal with them all. The primary motivation in relation to this compartment is love. While we might treat the various circles of our family life differently, we certainly don't want to project our cold and professional business demeanor to them. We have a different way of interacting with our friends and family than we do at work. We apply a different lens through which we relate to them—love.

For some, the family life compartment may overlap with another compartment we consider part of our "private life," our *spiritual life*. Spiritual life includes our relationship with God as well as with others in the church, and as with the family life compartment, here the primary motivation is love. God's love compels us to love. Indeed, those who follow Jesus are called our brothers and sisters in Christ, and we treat fellow believers to some extent like family. Since love is the motivation of both our family life and spiritual life, we tend to allow these spheres to work together more than we do the following two compartments.

The *work life* (or *business life*) compartment operates under a different set of rules than our spiritual and family lives, and thus we think of it differently. Being the breadwinner is serious stuff. There's no room to fool around. Even followers of Jesus often believe they must do whatever it takes to get ahead. It's a dog-eat-dog environment in which our spiritual life has no real place. And if not properly checked at the door, our faith might actually keep us from succeeding in our business life. We often justify the pursuit of financial success, power, and fame by a need to meet our family obligations. The need to care for our families certainly seems more noble than those other objectives, but it doesn't ultimately change what we're pursuing or how we're relating in our work life.

As with the business realm, the *political life* compartment seems characterized by anything but love. It's divisive. We're turned off by perceptions that politicians are tossed by the currents of polling results and will say anything to get elected. We may discuss politics at home, but not in public. Politics may jeopardize business relationships, and it has no place at church. Jesus would be above all that. Though this book doesn't delve into this area, I contend that our political life, like our business life, is often inappropriately compartmentalized from our spiritual life.

There are other compartments individuals have established, such as entertainment or sports and recreation lives. However, the ones described above are simply the four most common ones I see. Whatever the spheres, we've segmented our lives into compartments with little to no overlap. More to the point, our spiritual life is divorced from other important realms it should permeate, including our work life. Most of us never consciously intend this compartmentalization to happen, but it becomes an all-too-easy and all too common reality.

Messages of Compartmentalization

After committing my life to God, I was convinced there was no connection between faith and work. After all, those much more versed and professionally trained in the Bible never brought up the subject of work or business or even acknowledged there might be a value in it. That led to the impression that I could not truly serve God in business. Many of us who have been "churched" are left with a similar outlook.

My fellow believers in business reinforced the view that there's no intersection between work and faith. Only personal, relational, spiritual, or family matters were the subject of discussion or prayer. Nothing relating to their business lives was brought before God. Some significantly segregated their business lives from their church lives. I met business-men and -women who possessed strong business skills, but their attitudes and actions at work bore little resemblance to biblical norms. (Later I was shocked to find these same people in church.) Their lives at work simply operated under a different set of rules than what might be expected from a follower of Jesus. Faith and business don't mix.

So neither our business training nor our church train-ing offers a means for integrating faith and work. In fact, they both offer basic messages that reinforce the concept of keeping business and faith separate. Secular business school doesn't want us to sully business with spiritual pursuits, and church doesn't want us to sully our faith with business pursuits. And so we operate in very disconnected and very different worlds. We don't carry our faith to work. We go on leading our compartmentalized lives.

Our Compartmentalized Lives at Work

One reason we segment our work life from our spiritual life is the perception that they have irreconcilably different goals. If business schools preach the objective of profits, churches preach the objective of souls. These two objectives are liter-ally worlds apart. Believers in the marketplace typically acknowledge both goals as important, yet they have no way to reconcile the two.

I've observed three ways people usually deal with diver-gent business and spiritual goals. Maybe you can identify with one or more of these attitudes. If so, you're certainly not alone.

The Schizophrenic Believer in Business. One way to deal with the different objectives and attitudes found in our business world and our spiritual world is to live two lives. We become schizophrenic. There is a proper place for faith, but at work it's all about business objectives. Our business persona is tough, driven, competent, analytical, professional, savvy, and independent. Faith and strict adherence to biblical values would only interfere with business success. Better to leave that for church life. After all, business is business, right?

The Double-Minded Believer in Business. Another way to deal with the different objectives we perceive in our business life and our spiritual life is to devalue the one and covet the other. We become disillusioned with the unspiritual nature of secular work and yearn after work in ministry where our efforts would have more spiritual value. We become double-minded. The belief that our work is ultimately meaningless prevents us from fully engaging in our daily tasks, and we approach our work halfheartedly. We seek to minimize the demands of the business life compartment in order to maximize our time available to the spiritual life compartment. We dive into church activities and programs and may even desire to work for a Christian organization. After all, a spiritually committed person should serve God, right?

The Serial Believer in Business. Some of us deal with the different goals we perceive in the marketplace and the church by segmenting our lives into different phases or time periods. "I'll do ministry after I've made enough money," is a statement typical of this thinking. We tackle the business world first, seeking to achieve a certain level of success, prestige, or wealth. We may rationalize that these objectives are necessary to enable the second, more noble phase of our lives. Once successful, we shift gears, free to work for God in the ministry—to do something significant with our lives. Then we can really serve God, unencumbered by the struggles, stresses, and tensions of secular work. After all, we can't serve two masters, right?

Each of these three outcomes leaves us with a lack of integration between work and faith. The schizophrenic person sees no connection between work and faith and so conducts business in a way that has no relation to his faith. The double-minded person sees no connection between work and faith and so concludes service to God must take place outside the secular marketplace. The serial person sees no connection between work and faith and so concludes he should pursue business first and ministry later. Each of these is an expression of compartmentalization that keeps the walls of separation between spiritual life and business life firmly intact. And ultimately that leaves most of us with a deep sense that something's missing.

So we compartmentalize our work life and our spiritual life, you may be thinking, *but contrary to what you're suggesting, I think I can manage it. Is this issue really that serious?* In short, yes. Compartmentalization has a negative impact on the workplace, on the corporate church, and on the faith and work of individual believers.[8]

The Corporate Results of Compartmentalization

Impact on the Marketplace

As a result of compartmentalization, we fail to be salt and light in the marketplace. We're unprepared for and uninvolved in reaching others. The workplace isn't seen as the proper venue. If we're to influence others in the marketplace to become followers of Jesus, we need to take our faith to work.

When our faith is divorced from our work, we also fail to infuse industry with biblical values, practices, and views. By compartmentalizing God from our work life, we adopt wholesale the ethic of the marketplace without infusing it with the fragrance of Jesus. Even worse, some who separate work from faith tend to focus on what is legally defensible rather than on what is right in the eyes of God. The resulting marketplace suffers from a lack of personal trust and is marked by cold-hearted, self-seeking, or even corrupt business practices.

Impact on the Church

Compartmentalization harms the church's ability to reach those who aren't followers of Jesus, as the majority of the church's week is isolated from the effort to impact them. Compartmentalized thinking leads to the notion that the marketplace is not the venue for spiritual objectives. Rather, church is where spiritual objectives are to be pursued. Thus, we focus on reaching nonbelievers inside the walls of the church where the professionals reside. Our efforts are on bringing people to church rather than on bringing the church to the people. Meanwhile, to nonbelievers the church hardly seems like a place to go to find answers to their most pressing problems at work.

Compartmentalization also produces a faith that is marginalized from the bulk of our weekly activities. If God doesn't relate to our daily work and may not even care about it, we'll just check back on Sunday. Donald E. Wildmon, president of the American Family Association, wrote an essay titled "That's What Christians Do Now" in which he describes the prevailing attitude: "Me, I go to church, the minister preaches, I go home. That's what Christians do now." (See Appendix A for this powerful essay.) And the result of our faith being marginalized from the public square, of course, is that society reflects few biblical footprints.

The Personal Results of Compartmentalization

Impact on Our Faith and Family

On a personal level, compartmentalization also lessens our spiritual drive. If spiritual objectives are reserved for those working for churches, missions, and other religious organizations, then those of us in the marketplace are relieved of those responsibilities. We leave the heavy lifting to the professionals. As a result, our own spiritual muscles atrophy.

Compartmentalization also leaves us in a particularly unstable position. It will lead to one of two outcomes. Some of us will attempt to "do it all." Of course, that eventually leads to burnout, which leads to dropping out. Burned-out individuals have neither joy nor freedom, only feelings of hopelessness. Others will neglect important areas of their lives. Depending on which area seems to be the most meaningful or comfortable, we will ignore either family or business needs. Neglect of family can lead to divorce or a loss of relationships with children. Neglect of business or work can lead to lackluster performance and management feeling we're "not in the game," which at best leads to being passed over for promotions and at worst leads to losing our jobs.

Impact on Our Work

We may segregate our faith from our work to the extent that biblical morality and principles have no effect on our business dealings. We conduct business just like any person who doesn't claim to follow Jesus. We compromise our morals, we exhibit poor work ethics, we mistreat colleagues, we play power politics. These are all characteristics we seek to avoid in our personal and spiritual lives, but they represent our work life.

Christians in the marketplace who compartmentalize faith and business do not tap into the wealth of resources that are available. While issues in the church or at home may be routinely subjected to prayer, biblical inquiry, and guidance from the Holy Spirit, how often do we access these resources when conducting business? If we leave God out of our work, it's like we're running an eight-cylinder engine with only one sparkplug!

Compartmentalized living is not an option. It is unsustainable and leads to bad outcomes, both on corporate and individual levels. The Scripture calls us to a life of integrity.

A Lack of Integrated Oneness

The biggest single outcome of the compartmentalized life is a lack of integrity, or integrated oneness. In short, the compartmentalized life is the disintegrated life. When God works in different spheres, he isn't compartmentalized or divided; he exhibits integrated oneness. "All of God does all that God does," says A. W. Tozer.[9] So should we. But sadly, we suspend some attributes, abilities, and resources as we move from sphere to sphere. Compartmentalization is the very thing that weakens us.

I've come to realize that God wants us to lead integrated lives in which our faith influences every sphere, including our work in the marketplace. "There's no way we can compartmentalize our faith. We don't have any choice about it," says Larry Collett, EVP of Cass Commercial Bank. "We are integrated, consistent people. Therefore, the integration of our faith in the workplace should be as natural as it is at home, with our families, or at church. We should not be different people at different times and different places."[10] God asks us to be his agents of redemption in workplaces, neighborhoods, homes, societies, and congregations. He wants us to move from compartmentalization to integration.

On Balance and Integration

Whether we're in the marketplace or not, many of us are desperately seeking to balance our lives. Sadly for countless people, these two compartments compete with the others.

Love has few demands while work has many. We're conflicted between the different obligations and priorities in our lives, and there never seems to be enough time to get it all done.

The often less demanding compartments characterized by love (family life, spiritual life) compete with the more demanding work life compartment. Usually, the squeaky wheel gets the grease, while other parts of our life suffer. Trying to avoid this and keep all the balls in the air, we're in a constant state of fatigue, as we're running in overdrive.

Is Time Management the Answer?

Time management techniques are designed to maximize what time we do have available. But why do we want to gain all this time? Often, it's to do more of what we're already doing! To have more meetings, read more e-mails, and meet more customers. "The problem is time management techniques face the time problem at its point of greatest tension and claim to relieve that tension, but do so without requiring any radical break with our style of life," explains Robert Banks. "Time management techniques don't require us to challenge our fundamental views of time."[11] In short, time remains the idol that rules our life—time management is just an attempt to squeeze more out of it.

Sensing that our work is infringing too heavily on our personal and spiritual obligations, we're looking for ways to free up more time to "do more important stuff." I think all of us in the marketplace have felt at one point or another that our jobs have gotten in the way of things we really value, from attending Johnny's soccer game to serving in a church ministry to deepening relationships with friends and neighbors. Indeed, many of us would do well to find a different allocation of our limited time. But balance alone isn't enough. A balanced life can still be very compartmentalized. Let me explain.[12]

The measure of balance in life is time and priority: How much of my life is spent at work, and how much is spent on family, friends, faith, and community? And how should I be prioritizing these different areas of my life? Those pursuing better balance alone may succeed in reducing their work hours and increasing their family and ministry time, but that still leaves them with a sense that their work lacks spiritual value—or worse yet, that their business is being conducted on principles that run contrary to their faith. In fact, I've found that many business people who pursue balance never even consider whether their faith is truly integrated with their work or how it can be better integrated. They're simply looking for ways to reduce the time requirements of their jobs or somehow fit it all in.

By contrast, *the measure of integration in life is lordship*: How is every aspect of my life (work, family, friends, faith, community) a ministry of serving others to the glory of God? When you pursue integration, you're forced to consider the *how*, *what*, and *why* of your work, not simply the *when*. Rather than just writing off your work hours and seeking to minimize them, you will find ways for your faith to transform *how* you perform your work, to affect *what* you do at work, and to redefine *why* you work. You will give spiritual value to your time at work. The key to redeeming more of your time is to integrate, so that all spheres of your life move in the same direction, glorify the same God, and operate under the same values.

Balance or Integration?

Of course, there's no tradeoff between balance and integration. Balance without integration leaves us compartmentalized, while integration without balance leaves us without a sense of priority. We need both.

We need to make sure our lives are balanced—that we're committing the proper amount of time to each aspect of our lives in which God has called us to serve. We also need to make sure our lives are integrated—that we're thinking of and practicing each aspect of our lives as a ministry of serving others to the glory of God.

The Importance of Priorities and Balance

Many of our time problems are attributable to poor priorities or to poorly understood priorities. "We will gain more time by properly understanding [God's] will for us than by all the time-saving suggestions put together," notes Banks.[13] We need to undergo a radical reappraisal to reveal where we have strayed from the mission God has given us and let go of things that get in the way of pursuing it.

Priorities should be set up for our whole life, and our work is only one aspect of that. Our business has to fit into our life goals, not the other way around. When I started Inmac, I was faced with a decision regarding my personal involvement with the company. Entrepreneurs pursuing startup ventures notoriously pour their lives into the endeavor. God was teaching me that success could only be defined by a closer relationship with him ("Seek first his kingdom and his righteousness, and all these things will be given to you as well"—Matt. 6:33), my wife, and my kids ("If anyone does not provide for his relatives, and especially for his immediate family, he has denied the faith and is worse than an unbeliever"—1 Tim. 5:8), and only then by a successful business.

I realized I must be true to those priorities, not just pay lip service to them. As business people are inclined to do, I developed a plan. After calculating the number of waking hours in the week, I then considered time devoted to God. How many hours a week would be needed to ensure that I was growing in knowledge and intimacy with him? I repeated the exercise in order to set aside adequate time for my family. What remained in the week for work? Forty hours. (A similar analysis may not yield the same results for you, but the exercise is worth the effort.) I concluded that would have to be enough. They'd be an intense forty hours, but I reckoned God could make it work.

As you might surmise, my proposed forty-hour workweek wasn't well received by the venture capitalists I approached to fund our fledgling company. While they passed on investing in the business, I knew I was honoring God's priorities. (We ended up raising $50,000 from friends and family instead, and as a result of bootstrapping the startup venture, we ultimately maintained a greater equity interest in the company.) I gave the venture forty hours a week and did not work on the weekends. Mind you, those hours at work were intense, and I was forced to focus on the important. God was faithful to make the most of my efforts.

Having observed too many people who worked seventy hours a week for years only to burn out or to find their marriages end in divorce, I sometimes gave a speech to Inmac employees and fellow members of the business community titled "Why You Need to Work Only Forty Hours." It ran directly against the grain of Silicon Valley's conventional wisdom that says working longer and harder leads to success. I pointed out that a workaholic lifestyle is unsustainable in the long run. As we pursue personal heroics in the workplace, there's no margin for emergencies or reflection. And by making our business or career our overriding priority, we sometimes fail to make the rational, objective, and tough business decisions. I've seen people whose identity is so connected to their business that they don't recognize when they're pursuing a bad business concept. They simply cannot let go.

I hear people excuse their minimal time commitments to family, faith, and friends by saying, "I'm focused on spending quality time with them." I call it the "quality, not quantity" trap. In relationships, there is no quality without quantity.

I should also note that workaholism is not confined to the secular marketplace. Pastors and missionaries will report how overcommitted and busy their lives are. It's sometimes excused as "wholeheartedly serving God" or "putting God's work first," but workaholism is idolizing work whether it's in the church or in the marketplace. We need balance in our lives.

The Importance of Integration

Integration is another important pursuit, and it has a different, potentially more powerful effect on your life than balance. Think about how you can bring spiritual significance to more of your life. If you spend sixty hours per week on work-related activities (commuting, working, having lunch, thinking about work), that's about half your non-sleep time. The rest is available for stuff you deem spiritually or otherwise significant (faith, worship, family; perhaps even community, play, and friends).

Let's say you cut your working hours by two hours a workday, which many of us would consider a major coup. If you spend that time on activities you consider to have spiritual value, you've "redeemed" ten hours a week. But that noble effort to balance your life still leaves it compartmentalized. You still sense that the remaining fifty working hours have little or no spiritual significance.

Integration is the key to changing that mindset and thus "redeeming" the vast majority of your time, the hours devoted to work. When your work is a holy calling and a ministry, it's loaded with spiritual significance. All that time you spend at work has spiritual value. So while balance alone might redeem some hours, integration can redeem far more!

How Shall We Then Live?

What if we recognized a deep connection between faith and business? What if biblical values weren't roadblocks but actually the source of successful business? What if the real goal of business were more noble than profit maximization? What if we could see our everyday work as having spiritual value? What if we could approach it as ministry? What if it were our calling, a calling as high as that of a pastor or missionary? What if God cared deeply about our work and wanted to be involved? And what if we could even partner with him in our business? That's the paradigm of work and faith that forms the basis of the integrated life.

But how do we get out of this compartmentalization? That question is the beginning of a journey for many. It was for me. Many of us need to be retrained. We have adopted certain notions about the goal of business, the source of successful business practices, the ultimate value of secular work, the nobility of business, the meaning of ministry, the nature of a calling, and the role of the church. If we are to experience an integrated life, we need to reexamine these concepts. We need to be transformed by the renewing of our minds (Rom. 12:2). We need to adopt a new, biblical paradigm that connects faith and business.

Everything you learned in business school and church is wrong. Well, not really. But one of the reasons we compartmentalize our lives is that we operate on faulty tenets and beliefs that keep us from connecting our faith with our work. In the following sections, we will examine and correct key misconceptions on which our work–faith compartmentalization is built. Over the years, God has opened my eyes to more and more of these issues, and I suspect he's not done yet. But for now, here they are—what I didn't learn in business school and what I didn't learn in church.

PART II

What I Didn't Learn in Business School

I realize that many in the marketplace have not attended business school. (While business school was part of my experience, I am using the term *business school* as shorthand to connote our secular business training—from whatever source and in whatever setting.) This Part most certainly applies to everyone in the marketplace, whether your business education and job training may have taken place outside or inside the classroom. We've all gleaned information about conducting business.

The issues we're about to consider are profound. What is the real goal of business? (Chapter 4) What is the real source of successful business principles? (Chapter 5) And is there a relationship between economic prosperity and biblical values in a culture? (Chapter 6) Let's see if we can't make the biblical connection between faith and business that you won't find in business school.

CHAPTER 4

The Real Goal of Business

The paramount duty of management and of boards is to the corporation's stockholders.

(The Business Roundtable, 1997)

Many assume, wrongly, that a company exists simply to make money ... Profit is not the proper end and aim of management—it is what makes all of the proper ends and aims possible.

(David Packard, Cofounder,
Hewlett-Packard Company, 1942)

Serve wholeheartedly, as if you were serving the Lord, not men, because you know that the Lord will reward everyone for whatever good he does.

(St. Paul, AD 62)

Life Without Goals

A friend runs an organization that teaches life skills to kids all over the world through sports. One of the most important lessons is taught through an ingenious exercise.

The children are split into two teams, handed a soccer ball, and told to go play a game "over there" in an area of grass or dirt. They head out to play, but invariably, the kids soon return, visibly frustrated. "We can't play without lines on the field to mark the boundary," they complain. "And there aren't any goals, so we don't have anything to defend or shoot at!" That provides the opportunity for the lesson: Rules are important and good. We need boundaries and goals, whether in sports or in the game of life. And we need clearly defined objectives for our work as well.

What's It All About?

In 1996, a 17-year old girl in San Jose, California, scored a perfect 1,600 on the Scholastic Achievement Test and a perfect 8,000 on the difficult University of California Academic Index. Karen was the first person in history to accomplish this feat. Blessed with a brilliant mind, she was called "Wonder Woman" by her high school teachers because of her determined quest for knowledge and amazing ability to retain what she read. Karen's aspirations were to become a lawyer and then a judge, and who would doubt her ability to succeed? Her accomplishment made the national news. Seeking to plumb the depths of such an extraordinary intellect for wisdom, a reporter asked her, "What is the meaning of life?" Surely she'd have some brilliant insight.

"I have no idea," she responded. "I would like to know myself."[14]

Many of us feel the same way about business. We live it every day, but we really don't have a satisfactory answer to the question, "What is the goal of business?" We may believe that profits are important to companies, but is that the goal we should be pursuing? It's a significant question, as it shapes the way we think about our work and make decisions in business. So the purpose of this chapter is to explore the real goal of business. For many of us it will produce an important paradigm shift, a new way of looking at and conducting our business.

Business School: Maximize Shareholder Value

It's almost axiomatic today. Ask the average MBA what the goal of a corporation is, and he'll respond reflexively without thinking, "To maximize shareholder value." It's just about the first thing we learn in business school. Managers should seek to maximize shareholder wealth. And, of course, the best way to enrich the company's owners is to maximize the corporation's profits.

Now management teams certainly have an obligation to their investors, but if the shareholder is the sole constituent, it can be a recipe for cold, calculating dealings. Here's an example. In the name of maximizing profits for their investment partners, and thus for themselves, some private equity firms are buying troubled companies, plucking their valuable assets, and leaving the rest to rot. To be sure, large companies must streamline businesses and discontinue poor business segments in order to stay viable. But it doesn't seem these buyout shops have the long-term survival of their acquisitions as their overriding goal. Through "dividend recapitalizations" and "advisory fees," buyout shops extract billions of dollars in cash payments annually for their private equity investors. But to do so, they heavily mortgage the future of the companies they acquire. "Now and again corporate carnage follows, as thousands of employees lose their jobs, long-term prospects are diminished, and the business files for bankruptcy, stranding minority investors and debt holders," Forbes concludes.[15] Not a pretty picture, but the buyout firms maximized the return to their happy investors!

Stumbling in the Dark

So our secular business education leads us to the following as the lens through which all business decisions should be made: Does it maximize profits and provide the greatest benefit to the shareholders? But this leaves a lot of people inside and outside the business world with a level of discomfort. Is that really a noble objective?

Even secular business educators have sought to augment the maximizing-shareholder-value objective with something more redeeming. Some see a higher purpose in a company's vision or mission statement, which sometimes goes beyond growth goals to include values the company wants to reflect, such as a commitment to its employees, its customers, its community, or the environment. But even though the company's mission statement may include noble intentions toward various constituents, usually its ultimate goal is still profit maximization.

Uncomfortable with the overriding goal of maximizing shareholder value, some have suggested other objectives for business. Expanding the view beyond investors, we are to maximize stakeholder value, which includes benefits to employees, customers, and other constituents that relate to the business of the company. Another view is to focus on maximizing the value of the customer. Yet another is to maximize blended value, which considers a combination of economic, environmental, and social factors.

Who Says?

My son Kary recently completed an Executive MBA at Instituto de Empresa, the prestigious international business school in Madrid. In the ethics class discussion, one of the students laid out what his company does. This major international business has a department devoted entirely to making sure the business is responsive to all the various demands of "ethical responsibility." Finally, my son asked, "In competing responsibilities, how do you know which is the most important? And who determines what is right? Those who claim to take the greatest offense or complain the most? Those who attack you the most?" They had no answer.

Companies have no moral anchor, so they end up yielding to the pressure of "ethical responsibility" demanded by the most powerful groups. The real issue is this: Who says? Are business objectives and responsibilities determined by a group that happens to be loud and has a certain amount of popular backing, or are they determined by some higher authority, such as God?

Missing the Goal

Whether the stated goal is maximizing stakeholder value, the value of the customer, or some sort of blended value of economic, environmental, and social factors, these all suffer from a problem that also plagues the maximize-shareholder-value goal: they're not capable of being acted on, and they conflict with the concept of maximizing shareholder value. They don't tell us what to do. How do we go about our work of maximizing stakeholder value or blended value on any given day? How do we even measure it? These are noble attempts to cure some of the problems resulting from purely profit-oriented decision making, but in the end they're neither strategies nor practicable objectives.

They're also pursuing by-products, as they focus on secondary effects. What I mean is this: If our work is properly aligned with the right goal, we will be taking care of shareholders and customers and employees in the course of doing business. It's like saying our primary obligation in life is to help the poor. Yes, Jesus commanded us to do so, but he also gave us the greatest command, our overriding obligation in life: "'Love the Lord your God with all your heart and with all your soul and with all your mind.' This is the first and greatest commandment. And the second is like it: 'Love your neighbor as yourself'" (Matt. 22:37–39). If we are following these commandments, we'll be compelled to help the poor. Helping the poor is a secondary effect, a by-product of pursuing our primary goal.

The Real Goal of Business: Serve Others to the Glory of God

So is there a similar overriding goal for business out of which flow all these redeeming by-products? I think so, and it's the first thing I didn't learn in business school. The real goal of business is simply this: to serve others to the glory of God.

Note that this objective places one's business activity squarely within the overriding command Jesus gave us for life—to love God with everything we have and to love our neighbors—our fellow humans—as we love ourselves. Part of the reason so many of us find the need to compartmentalize our lives is that we're pursuing different objectives in different spheres. But if our goal in business is to serve others to the glory of God, our work assumes spiritual value and the objectives of our professional life and personal life converge.

J. C. Penney, who founded one of the most successful retail chains of the 20th century, recognized that serving others gives business spiritual value. He explained this insight to the public in an early store ad: "The assumption was that business is secular, and service is religious. I have never been able to accept that line of arbitrary demarcation ... Is not service part and parcel of business? It seems to me so; business is therefore as much religious as it is secular. If we follow the admonition to love God, and our neighbors as ourselves, it will lead us to understand that, first of all, success is a matter of the spirit."[16] Penney's overarching objective in business was serving others to the glory of God, and that imbued his work with spiritual value.

What About Profits?

Note that I'm not implying profitability is an unnecessary or unworthy aim. There are three reasons why profits are a key part of serving others to the glory of God:

1. *We need to recognize that business that effectively serves others will generate value and expand the total pie.* Profit is a sign that others are being served effectively, not that advantage is being taken of them.
2. *Business cannot neglect efficiency and profitability or it will cease being able to serve others.* The value statement of A. G. Edwards & Sons, a brokerage and investment firm, reads, "Profit is not the purpose of our business and should not be sought after for its own sake. Rather, it is a necessity if we are to be able to continue to deliver value to our clients."[17] Profit is required to keep a business alive and expand its capacity to serve others, much as tithes and offerings are necessary to keep a church running and expand its capacity to serve others.
3. *Serving investors means that we'll generate a return on their investment.* In Jesus' parable of the talents (see Matt. 25:14–30), the servant who generates a profit for his master is highly commended for his faithful service.

When Inmac opened a manufacturing plant in East Kilbride, Scotland, a major semiconductor company was closing theirs in the area and moving operations to a lower-cost country. All our new employees had that on their minds. As the CEO, I was at the manufacturing plant to greet these wonderful people, welcome them to the company, and answer any questions. We all met on the manufacturing floor to discuss our bright future together. The Scots, not ones to mince words, asked, "When will you close the doors and move to a lower-cost country? How long will you keep this plant open?"

Al Cotton, my very wise Vice President of Human Resources, answered, "As long as you continue to find ways to reduce the cost of our products so that we can provide competitive, high-quality products which provide us with a profit and thus the ability to stay open here." Our employees thought about that and said that was fair.

During all the years I remained with the company, the workers in East Kilbride continued to reduce costs and provide high quality products through innovative design and work layout. People on the factory floor even took orders for custom products and could give the customer the correct prices, manufacturing, and delivery dates, as they knew the costs and daily production schedules intimately. They could fit specials in without missing a beat. Since we did not need a customer service representative or cost estimator, we saved both expense and potential confusion. In short, they served others effectively. The plant continued to provide quality products that generated a profit, thus allowing the workers in East Kilbride to continue to serve customers and the rest of the company.

So profit is a necessary condition of serving others effectively, but it's not the goal of business. It's like oxygen in running a race. A runner needs oxygen to win. In the process of running the race, he breathes deliberately. His objective is to finish first, to outrun his opponents. It's not to maximize his breathing or take in more oxygen than the next guy. But if he's going to win, he needs to have his breathing figured out. Effective breathing is necessary for running a great race. Similarly, the goal of a business should be to serve others, not to maximize its profits. But in the process of serving others, there will be opportunity for profit. Profitability is a by-product of serving others effectively, and it is necessary for the business to continue or even expand its service. "Seek first his kingdom and his righteousness and all these things will be given to you as well," Jesus instructed (Matt. 6:33).

What Does "Serving Others" Imply?

If serving others to the glory of God is to be the hallmark of what we do in business, then it should permeate every activity. We must serve all those God brings before us in business.

The most obvious application of this principle relates to customer interactions. The commands of Jesus provide a helpful guide for excellent service to customers: "do to others as you would have them do to you" and "love your neighbor as yourself." Serving others means asking the question, "How would I want to be treated in this situation?" I'm sure all of us can think of a time when we've experienced truly excellent service—and plenty of times when we didn't!

What does service mean in the context of managing people? Taking the example of Jesus, leaders are to be servants to their group. They are not to give up their leadership, but they are to manage with an attitude of service. I know that's contrary to the common heroic leadership style found in organizations today. We're all familiar with managers who exert the power of their position, emphasize their superiority in the organizational hierarchy, and segregate themselves from their underlings. The Bible's instruction is to "serve one another in love" (Gal. 5:13). Even leaders, and I'd say especially leaders, are to operate with a servant's heart.

Sometimes serving others means recognizing when their real needs are different than their perceived needs. Management teams are often inclined to take shortcuts in the interest of satisfying shareholders, as short-term profits are emphasized over long-term success of the business. However, truly serving investors would mean recognizing that their real need is a company that is making healthy profits well into the future, not just today.

I have encountered another situation where the perceived need may not be the real need—when an employee is failing in his job and needs to be let go. Serving the employee means doing what you can to help him succeed, but occasionally a person simply does not have the capability to perform a job. Though he may not recognize it at the time, he's being served by being released from failure to pursue another position more suited to his abilities. Of course, we need to have an attitude of love in what is a most stressful situation for all concerned. But almost every person I've had to let go later thanked me for recognizing a poor fit with the demands of the position and for opening the door to find a place where he or she could succeed. Serving others may mean making difficult decisions that are not popular.

Sometimes truly serving others means discerning and addressing latent needs. Chuck Ripka cofounded Riverview Community Bank in Otsego, Minnesota, a kingdom-focused business designed to minister to people in the community. The rapidly growing bank exceeded its own asset and income projections almost two years ahead of plan. When customers come to the bank, the staff ask if there's anything they can pray about. Word has spread, and people have driven up to three hours to visit "the bank that prays with people." Ripka explains, "The attitude of management is that if a customer is struggling to make his payments on time, we are not going to send out the collectors, but we will call him to ask how we can pray for his situation."[18] Riverview Community Bank is going well beyond the obvious financial services needs before them to discern and meet people's latent needs for God's help. They're truly serving others to the glory of God.

What Does "to the Glory of God" Imply?

There are several implications of doing our work to the glory of God. The first is that our work must be in harmony with God's creational purposes. God commands us to fill the earth and rule over His creation. This includes development of the world through the creation of useful products and the delivery of useful services. Some business activities and realms, such as pornography or illegal drugs, do not fulfill his mandate. But most commercial activities, from producing medical equipment to dry cleaning to selling groceries to farming, are helpful to society.[19]

Second, if our work is done to the glory of God, it should be done with excellence. "Whatever you do, work at it with all your heart, as working for the Lord, not for men" (Col. 3:23). Paul was addressing slaves in this verse. God cares about the work we do, no matter how insignificant it seems. John Calvin put it this way: "No task will be so sordid and base, provided you obey your calling in it, that it will not shine and be reckoned very precious in God's sight."[20]

Others also notice the quality of our work and often view it as a reflection of our faith. Sadly, I've witnessed Christians whose work ethic and performance do not bring glory to God in the eyes of their co-workers. Whether its source is laziness or a misguided view that work in the marketplace has no spiritual value, poor work neither serves others nor brings glory to God. On the other hand, I know many followers of Jesus who perform their work with excellence, well beyond what's expected. In doing so, they prove to be a real inspiration to the whole team and bring glory to God.

God's Definition of Success

Our society measures personal success in a number of ways from material possessions to power to status. In business, it's the size and growth of your company and your rank in the organization that counts. But God's not concerned with that. In his economy, personal success has nothing to do with who earns the most, manages the largest group, or climbs the ladder the quickest. He's concerned with our hearts and relationships. He measures success by the degree to which we're serving others to his glory in the sphere to which he has called us. It's about being the best possible servant to others. Whether you're called to work in a business, a church, a school, or a home, success is serving others to the glory of God. So the question to ask is, "How can I follow my calling and serve in a better, larger, or more significant way?" If that's our objective in business, I believe the chances of meeting our society's definition of success also improve.

But pursuing this goal is not a guaranteed recipe for earthly success. There will be times when doing the right thing and truly serving others will have negative economic consequences. The Christian owner of a U.S. car dealership analyzed his sales data and made a discovery that irked his sense of justice. Women and minorities were less persistent or adept in the bargaining process and thus ended up paying more on average than others, who tended to be more affluent and educated. He resolved to remedy the inequity by offering only fixed prices to all customers. "I am Christian," he told his staff. "I believe we have to be willing to sacrifice some financial profit in order to fulfill justice." There was consistent agreement within the organization, even among those who weren't followers of Jesus.

As a result of the revised sales model, the dealership saw its profits drop ten percent. The owner and employees discussed whether they should revert back to the old model in light of the economic impact, but they concluded that what they were doing was right. They'd continue the practice of fixed prices and look to improve the bottom line in other ways. After months of implementing best practices and bettering their efficiency and effectiveness, the dealership improved its profitability by five percent. They never did achieve the same profit levels as before, but the dealership was filled with employees proud of what the company was doing.[21] We need to be willing to follow God's precepts, even if they result in failure by society's standard, because in God's eyes success is being faithful to his call.

There is a second important thing I didn't learn in business school. It's a grave omission in traditional business education, and like the teaching on the goal of business, it too often promotes compartmentalization. It is the failure to identify the real source of successful business practices.

CHAPTER 5

Where Do Business Principles Come From?

The citizen is a better businessman if he is a Christian gentleman and, surely, business is not the less prosperous and successful if conducted on Christian principles.

(U.S. President Grover Cleveland, 1837–1908)

Honesty is the best policy; but he who is governed by that maxim is not an honest man.
(Richard Whately, Archbishop of Dublin, 1787–1836)

Every young man would do well to remember that all successful business stands on the foundation of morality.

(Henry Ward Beecher, 1813–1887)

Finding Gold on the Dirt Road

If someone who knew nothing about the origins of gold were walking down a dirt road and his foot struck a large, glittering gold nugget, he'd be ecstatic at his discovery. Wow, what an amazing and valuable find! He'd take it home, treasure it, and perhaps sell it. But based on this experience, he might also have developed a very faulty view of the source of gold. His discovery would lead him to believe that gold comes from dirt roads rather than from veins in rock deposits. So where do you think he would look for more gold? That's right—on dirt roads.

This is exactly the situation with our secular business schools and their view of successful business principles. Truth is truth no matter where you find it, and indeed, business schools have discovered some truths in their work. But they don't recognize that those truths have their origins in the Bible. They fail to identify the biblical source of the principles that lead to successful business. Thus, our training misses the deep connection of Scripture to our work and the reason why these business principles work. And that leads many of us to compartmentalize our work and our faith.

So the second thing I didn't learn in business school is that good business principles didn't originate in the halls of academia; they are in fact biblical principles. There are a lot of biblical values business schools won't touch or teach, and these, likewise, prove to be successful business principles. There's a fundamental connection between biblical principles and successful capitalism.

Many business people who operate on biblical principles are successful—and not in spite of following them. They are successful *because* they follow them. The Scriptures are highly relevant to successful business. Now I'm not telling you to withdraw that secular business school application and instead enroll in seminary for a business education. Business schools have distilled a lot of truth into useful lessons. But we'll see there's a connection between sound business practices and the timeless values and principles of Scripture. We'll discover that gold actually comes from veins in the rock, not from the dirt road.

The Moral Foundation of Business

In 1993, the Nobel Prize in Economics was awarded to Dr. Douglass North for his work on institutional economics. His conclusions have very quietly revolutionized economic thinking. Dr. North proved a direct link between long-term successful economic development and certain institutions in society. What does "institution" mean in this context? It is the codification of values as broad agreements among a whole population—in other words, the accepted norms for regulating the society's commerce and other activities, such as politics. Dr. North proved that a society's formal rules of the political system (constitutions, laws, regulations) and informal rules of the moral-cultural system (morals, conventions, social norms) lay the foundation for its economic performance.

But on what kind of morality does capitalism tend to thrive?[22] *Amorality* is becoming more and more the predominant moral foundation in the Western world today. The question is not whether something is right or wrong but whether it's legal or illegal. The legal system takes the place of personal morality and values, and anything that is legally defensible is acceptable. When business is conducted from an amoral foundation, trust and loyalty are foreign concepts. Promises can be broken "when necessary" if there's no legally binding contract. Lawyers find loopholes and devise maneuvers around inconvenient laws. The result is a cold, calculating, and bleak business environment in which employees find very little comfort and customers operate in suspicion of the fine print.

Where there is no trust, there is a greater need for oversight, for laws, for legal checks and balances. In 2002, a reaction to corporate scandals at Enron, WorldCom, and other companies resulted in regulations named after U.S. Senators Sarbanes and Oxley which require public corporations to demonstrate oversight and fraud-prevention procedures. The noble intentions were to protect shareholders, but these new checks and balances now cost the average company an additional $1.3 million per year![23] Legislation is becoming more and more complex, as it seeks to codify into law the "right" businesses should be doing. The cost of this oversight increases the price of doing business and puts the nation at an economic disadvantage. But it's the only way to effect a change in behavior in an amoral environment where people are concerned about what's legal rather than what's right. An amoral environment leads to a libertine environment and eventually to a third-world environment where every person is for himself and the system of economics begins to break down.

A business environment that operates according to a *moral* standard provides the decidedly best foundation. People and companies exhibit values such as service, integrity, and loyalty because they are morally right, not because the law mandates them. (It does not.) Unique business problems are not ruled by law but by what is right for all concerned in the situation. Individuals are not simply equated with their perceived contribution to the bottom line; they are considered to have intrinsic value. The human spirit thrives in a moral business environment. When others are known to operate under an absolute moral standard, trust follows. And where there is full trust, handshakes replace lengthy contracts. There is less need for security, oversight, and checks. Transactions are simplified, and the cost of doing business decreases.

Following God's Moral Standard

President Theodore Roosevelt believed, "To educate a person in mind and not in morals is to educate a menace to society." Former SEC Chairman John Shad was alarmed by the number of graduates of leading business schools who were involved in the corporate scandals of the 1980s. So he offered to donate $20 million to his alma mater, Harvard Business School to establish an ethics program. But first, with an initial gift of $250,000, the school would need to define "ethics" and what would be taught.

What unfolded at Harvard Business School could have happened at any of the leading institutions. "After months of contentious debate," an observer notes, "an initial proposal was put up for a faculty-wide vote. As a visiting professor, I was sitting in the bleachers—and I witnessed a memorable scene. Reactions ranged from distrust to outright hostility. One economist argued that 'we are here to teach science.' Another faculty member wanted to know, 'Whose ethics, what values, are we going to teach?' And a third pointed out that the students were adults who got their ethics education at home and at church. By meeting's end, the project had been sent back to the drawing board."[24] John Shad's millions never did go toward an ethics department.

Note the faculty's implicit compartmentalization in the arguments that they're teaching a science and that ethics belong to one's family life or spiritual life. It was a far cry from the attitude adopted at the school's founding in 1908. When an early Harvard Business School donor requested that a course on ethics be included in the curriculum, Harvard's president at the time, Lawrence Lowell, replied that the subject should be included in each course as "an integral part of the principles that are explained."[25]

Indeed, many Christian business schools reflect the approach to business education he suggests. My friend John Mulford is former Dean of the Graduate School of Business at Regent University, a Christian college. When asked once whether the school had an ethics course, he responded that it did not, because every class considers business issues in light of biblical wisdom and instruction. Every class is an ethics class.

Note also the dilemma of the relativist with a postmodern worldview: "Whose ethics, what values, are we going to teach?" What should be the source of a moral standard for society in general and business in particular? Many are stumped. A professor at a top business school instructed his "Business Ethics" class to read a case study about Braniff, a troubled airline headed toward bankruptcy. Hearing Braniff was in financial difficulty, a customer called the CEO. He wanted to buy a large number of tickets. But would the airline still be flying in a couple of months? the customer wanted to know. According to the case, Braniff's CEO replied that he wasn't sure. The students argued that the head of the company represented the shareholders and thus should have lied. The CEO was jeopardizing the sale and thus shareholder equity by being honest.

Unsure how to proceed, the teaching professor went to an associate dean for advice. The dean was at a loss himself and arranged for a faculty conference to discuss the matter. At the meeting, a number of justifications for lying were brought forth. Some professors argued business is like poker—you have to bluff sometimes; it's part of the game. Others took a utilitarian point of view, stating that what is moral is that which yields the greatest aggregate benefit. Thus, lying was the correct course of action, because the alternative might have led to the airline's collapse, harming shareholders, employees, and creditors.

There were some who argued for truth-telling, albeit on the basis of self-interest. Those found lying in business, they noted, will lose customers; those who are honest will get more business. Thus, telling the truth was a good idea in this case. "Only two faculty members insisted that telling the truth is an absolute moral value and that the CEO should therefore avoid lying," reported a visiting instructor of ethics at the school. "The professor returned to his classes, as many others did, with a reinforced sense that teaching ethics was a tricky business and that one should not take a firm position in favor of one value or another. It all depends ..."[26] Since there's no consensus on the basis for morality in business, many opt for the final choice—none of the above.

Self-Interest: The Prevailing Moral Standard

What are the options for a moral standard in business? Some note that the business world rewards those who are perceived to operate morally and thus advocate *self-interest* as the moral standard. Do what is right, because it's in your best interest. Honesty is the best policy, because it yields the best results. Self-interest is often the de facto source of morality found in business. It's also a very convenient standard for morality: that which is in my best interest is also morally right.

A significant problem with self-interest as the basis for moral behavior is that it's ambiguous. Some argued Braniff's CEO should lie and others that he should tell the truth, both appealing to self-interest. Self-interest is a short-term, suboptimized best, so a morality based on self-interest is also subject to change. Promises will be broken when the alternative offers the potential of a greater return. Honesty will be abandoned as soon as it appears not to be in one's best interest, when it appears not to be the best policy. Courses of action are carefully weighed on a cost-benefit basis.

Business school students were asked whether they would attempt an illegal act that would net them or their company a profit of more than $100,000 if there were a one percent chance they'd be caught and sent to prison for a year. Computing the expected cost and benefit, more than one-third said they would.[27] Ultimately, self-interest results in situational ethics that are guided by the degree of personal gain. It proves a poor standard for morality in business.

God's Revealed Moral Standard

By contrast, a robust moral culture is formed when the *higher authority of God* is the source of ethical standards. Rather than appealing to a changeable morality based on self-interest, followers of the Judeo-Christian faith operate on immutable truths. They choose honesty not because it's the best policy but because it's the *only* policy, God's policy. They choose loyalty and fairness not simply because it's in their best interest; they do so because they are ultimately accountable to an almighty God. They do so because their consciences have been transformed by his word. Lord Brian Griffiths concludes that the Judeo-Christian faith "which sees business as a vocation or calling, so that a career in business is perceived as a life of service before God, is a most powerful source from which to establish, derive, and support absolute moral standards in business life."[28] When followers of Jesus heed the call to be holy in all they do, they're subject to a higher moral authority. Their moral foundation is defined and absolute.

The Biblical Values of Successful Business

Personal character was touted as the overriding success factor in the first 150 years of the United States, notes Stephen Covey, author of the popular book *The Seven Habits of Highly Successful People*. Benjamin Franklin and others espoused virtues such as integrity, temperance, humility, courage, and fidelity. In the last 50 years, notes Covey, that character ethic has been replaced by a personality ethic. One's outside appearance is now deemed more important than what's inside. Success is seen as a function of dressing right, understanding corporate politics, speaking eloquently, and excelling in social situations. But personal character is no less a success factor than before, as Covey and others are rediscovering. Character is the long-lost ingredient of successful capitalism, and biblical values rather than techniques or mental attitudes remain the underlying values of the character ethic.

I have come to recognize that the Bible is an important source of the values and principles of successful business. God has a lot to say about what traits should mark a follower of Jesus: integrity/honesty/truthfulness, loyalty/faithfulness, trust, commitment, order/cleanliness, hope. He has a lot to say about what should characterize our interactions with our fellow man: humility, service, respect/dignity, justice/fairness, grace/compassion, forgiveness, consideration, trust, accountability, interdependence, love. And he has a lot to say about the qualities that should describe our work: service, excellence, diligence, value, quality. I've listed these along with their scriptural directives in Appendix B.

You will find some of these values lauded by business scholars, but others are rarely if ever addressed in business education. Some are captured in the law of the land, but most are not. As Jesus taught, our actions are to go well beyond what's mandated by the legal code—even in business.

Think of the story of the Good Samaritan as an example of going beyond the law to do what is right. The secular person wants to limit responsibility (what's my minimum legal obligation?) while the biblical person wants to go beyond it (what's right in the eyes of God?). The personal character values, interpersonal relationship values, and performance values Scripture prescribes most definitely apply to and are sorely needed in the marketplace.

Business Under the Gold Standard

Many believers operate under the faulty assumption that they can't afford to act according to biblical attitudes and values at work. Aren't those who operate morally playing against a stacked deck? This view is often promoted in the marketplace, and it's even reinforced explicitly or implicitly in the church. I've seen many reports about successful business people who employ biblical principles, and the prevailing theme is usually one of incredulity. Wow, this person succeeded despite the albatross of following God's laws! How could he or she possibly make it without cutting corners, engaging in dishonesty, and treating employees dispassionately?

We really need to rethink that point of view. Business success that results from following biblical principles should not be surprising. President Grover Cleveland said, "Business is not the less prosperous and successful if conducted on Christian principles," as we will see in the following story.

The Golden Rule Stores

In 1902, Kemmerer, Wyoming, was a small mining community of about 1,000 people. Like the 21 saloons in town, the established dry goods store sold mostly on credit, leaving many heavily indebted to the company store. It was customary to haggle over prices, as the clerks sought to extract the most from each customer; some in the community were treated a bit more fairly than others in the process.

Next door to this business, a 26-year old and his new wife set up shop in a smaller run-down building, also intending to sell dry goods. The couple had capital and inventory only one-sixteenth that of the larger competitor, but they set out to do business in a radically different way, as evidenced by the shop's name: the Golden Rule Store. "Do to others as you would have them do to you," was Jesus' famous command (Luke 6:31) that formed the basis for service in the business. The Golden Rule Store had prominently displayed fixed prices that were available to every customer who entered the door. It sold on a cash-only basis, and while this required customers to budget for purchases, it also lowered their price and kept them free from indebtedness.

The Golden Rule Store flourished and became a model for future success. Within a decade, thirty more Golden Rule Stores were opened. By 1913, unscrupulous competitors had seen the value of the Golden Rule name and began to adopt it. Thus the company changed its name to reflect the name of its founder, J. C. Penney. But there was no less emphasis on following biblical precepts. The Penney Idea, a mission statement adopted at the first company meeting that year had as the last of its seven goals "To test our every policy, method, and act in this wise: 'Does it square with what is right and just?'" The Golden Rule remained a guiding principle of the company.

At a time when shoddy products were being peddled and merchant attitudes often reflected their monopoly status in town, the Golden Rule Store stood in stark contrast to the prevailing *caveat emptor* (let the buyer beware) business mentality. Not only was value being offered in terms of quality and price, James Cash Penney insisted on the most courteous service as the basis of any transaction. Penney referred to the Golden Rule as essentially the Rule of Service, and he was explicit and open about the role his Christian faith played in bringing God's principles of value and service to bear in the marketplace.

J. C. Penney was also deeply committed to his employees, rewarding, training, and developing them to use their gifts. As the company grew to several stores, he instituted a profit-sharing plan, another practice radical for the time and informed by his faith. All his employees were thus associates. Some of them also bought in as partners when successive stores were opened in new locations. Promising employees became store clerks and were later given the opportunity to buy into new expansion stores.

James Cash Penney inherited many biblical principles from three generations of Baptist-preacher ancestors, and he integrated these into his business ventures. "To me the sign on the store was much more than a trade name," recounted Penney. "In setting up a business under the name and meaning of the Golden Rule, I was publicly binding myself, in my business relations, to a principle which had been a real and intimate part of my family upbringing," he noted. "The Golden Rule finds no limit of application in business."[29] Penney credited a commitment to this biblical principle with the success of his stores.

Business people may scoff at the application of "unproven" biblical nuggets of gold in the marketplace. To many it seems like fool's gold. "Shrewd merchants and bankers laughed at Penney's Golden Rule ethics, predicting his prompt failure, especially since Penney insisted on cash-and-carry," notes one historical account of his start in retailing.[30] Even when the business case wasn't obvious, J. C. Penney was uncompromising in allowing biblical values to form and differentiate his business, trusting God for the outcome. While operating against the common wisdom of the day, Penney had stellar success and changed the rules of store merchandising to this day. He was a man whose faith deeply infused his work.

Business success doesn't require us to leave our faith at the door. In fact, biblical principles are foundational to successful capitalism. Having said that, I am not advocating that we practice these principles on the basis of self-interest—in other words, merely because they produce good economic outcomes. They should be practiced in submission to an almighty God who revealed them as immutable truth. When we seek the Bible's instruction and wisdom, we're looking for gold nuggets in the right place. When we apply these nuggets in our work, we'll be led to God's best for us.

Douglass North showed that the internalization of biblical values in a culture leads to more business success, but how exactly does that happen? Does it really matter in the grand scheme of things whether we exhibit biblical principles in business? And how do we reconcile the continued economic success in the Western world with the fact that biblical values are less and less prevalent in the marketplace? These questions lead me to the third thing I didn't learn in business school.

CHAPTER 6

Spiritual Capital: The Missing Leg of the Stool

Wealth creation requires capital investment, and perhaps the most important part of that investment is the spiritual capital from which enterprise actually begins.

(Dr. Theodore Roosevelt Malloch, 2006)

If we learn anything from the history of economic development, it is that culture makes almost all the difference.

(Harvard Professor David Landes, 2000)

Christian faith and Christian values set the foundation for successful business. Without the power of the gospel changing the hearts and minds of our people, [South Korea] would not have witnessed the same economic blessing.

(Dr. David Yonggi Cho, 2005)

The Capitals of Business

One of the axioms of business is that you need to start with capital. When you hear the term "capital," what comes to mind? Most often it evokes thoughts of cash. You may have heard the statement, "You've gotta spend money to make money." But there are other forms of capital that are essential in business and society. In business school we learn that if we're going to start or operate a venture, we need money (economic capital), relationships (social capital), and skill sets (cultural capital). Indeed, we are taught that these are the types of capital that drive an economy.

What I didn't learn in business school is that another form of capital has economic function and is critical to economic development: spiritual capital. In fact, I have come to realize that it's the unrecognized pillar of capitalism, the essential oil that makes an economic system run.

What is spiritual capital? Think of it as the faith, trust, and commitment to do what is right in the eyes of God—show integrity, be accountable, be honest, offer hope, love others, be trustworthy, exhibit good stewardship, be fair, create order, be loyal, and serve others.[31] In other words, spiritual capital produces the belief that others will exhibit the biblical values we spoke of in the last chapter, most of which go well beyond what's required by the laws of the land.

Spiritual Capital: The Key to Economic Blessing

Like the other types of capital mentioned above, spiritual capital is critical to economic success. Dr. Theodore Malloch calls it "the missing leg in the stool of economic development."[32] He's spot on. Spiritual capital is the trust that others will do what's right in the eyes of God, and that produces far more fertile ground for business.

Remember the work of Douglass North (Chapter 5), whose Nobel-winning work uncovered the factors that characterize successful economies? This trust factor, when pervasive in a society, is one of the "institutions" of which Dr.

North speaks—institutions that lead to a better economy. Other institutions include hope, honesty, respect, accountability, integrity, rule of law, and property rights—all biblical values that build spiritual capital. These moral-cultural values directly affect the level of success of a society, a point the Nobel Committee believed he proved conclusively.

Think about the economic implications if there were no spiritual capital and thus no trust. Say a consumer wants to buy a chicken to eat. The buyer could literally spend half a day making the purchase. First, he will certainly want to *see* the chicken. Then comes the bargaining. No established price exists, since the seller wants to get as much as he can for each chicken. He starts by asking far more than the chicken is worth. Maybe he can get this buyer to pay more than the last one did? The buyer wonders what information the seller is withholding about the chicken. The seller claims it's a healthy bird, but those statements often do not correspond to reality, and the buyer has no recourse. Will this bird prove to have a disease that makes his family sick when it's consumed?

A lack of trust can turn a simple transaction like purchasing a chicken into a horrendously costly exercise, never mind more complex transactions. By contrast, where much spiritual capital is present, others are given the benefit of the doubt, and transaction costs are lower. This has profound implications on the development, success, and culture of an economy.

At the beginning of the twentieth century, one of the founders of sociology examined the origins of successful capitalism. Why, asked Max Weber, did capitalism thrive in certain parts of Europe and especially in the United States? His conclusion was simple and powerful. He noted that predominantly Protestant nations had adopted values of vocation, hard work, and personal piety that led to greater economic success. Neighboring countries with similar resources and people groups didn't fare as well. Weber noted that in Catholic societies, the pious served in the Church; in Protestant cultures, the spirit of personal piety permeated into the marketplace and built spiritual capital. Applying internalized biblical values to business resulted in successful capitalism.[33] Almost a century apart, Max Weber and Douglass North reached very similar conclusions—that a society's beliefs and values are strong determinants of its economic success.

Indeed, it is interesting to observe that with very few exceptions, every nation at the top of the GDP-per-capita list has a long Judeo-Christian tradition. That's no coincidence. There's a relationship between economic prosperity and the pervasiveness of biblical values in the culture. And the concept of spiritual capital explains why that's the case. When biblical principles are practiced in business, spiritual capital grows, and economic success follows. Thus, spiritual capital provides the link between biblical principles and business success.

The lack of recognition of spiritual capital's importance has led to disastrous outcomes. For example, it has been thought for decades that the world's financial community holds the keys to success for developing nations. What's holding back certain regions of the world, the argument goes, is a lack of access to economic capital. Bangladesh has been the focus of the largest microenterprise development programs. More than 10 million people have received business loans over the past thirty years, yet poverty is still pervasive, and the economy hasn't developed much. Why? Bangladesh also suffers from the highest perceived corruption in the world. Development efforts provided economic capital but not the tools to build the nation's spiritual capital.

Likewise, billions of dollars have been invested in African economies, but it hasn't made a dent. In fact, economic data suggests these nations are worse off today than they were before they received funding from the West. "Most African nations today are poorer than they were in 1980, sometimes by very wide margins," note Haber, North, and Weingast. "More shocking, two-thirds of the African countries have either stagnated or shrunk in real per capita terms since the onset of independence in the early 1960s."[34] Much of the money disappeared and is suspected to reside in the Swiss bank accounts of various corrupt leaders and dictators. Where funds did reach the local economy, they failed to achieve any sustained economic growth. The large-scale attempts to reform African economies fell flat because they focused on the lack of economic capital and poverty but did nothing about the woeful lack of spiritual capital so evident in the marketplace.

The Spiritual Capital Account

But why do we continue to see economic success in the West when biblical values are less and less on display in the marketplace? We need to understand that at the individual and corporate levels, spiritual capital accrues as in an account. The spiritual capital account is developed one transaction at a time, and each interaction either increases or decreases it. When an employee is treated with respect and love, when an agreement is honored even though it proves costly, when a customer is served with integrity, when a product's quality exceeds expectations, when an employer is afforded loyalty and commitment—these biblical values applied to business serve to increase the spiritual capital account. Likewise, there are any number of dishonest, inconsiderate, and unbiblical business practices that reduce the spiritual capital account.

In 2006, the World Bank published a comprehensive analysis of the source of wealth in nations. The study determined how much of a nation's wealth can be attributed to natural resources (e.g., oil, minerals, cropland, pastures, forests) and produced capital (e.g., buildings, machinery, equipment, urban land). These are what we typically think of as "capital." The rest of the wealth is attributable to intangible factors such as the degree of trust, skill of labor, clarity of property rights, effectiveness of government, and efficiency of the judicial system. An amazing 80 percent of the wealth in rich countries is actually this intangible capital. The United States has $418,000 of intangible capital and $95,000 of natural and produced capital per person. By comparison, in neighboring Mexico, the average person has $34,000 of intangible capital and $28,000 of natural and produced capital.[35]

The World Bank furthermore sought to determine what drives the value of this intangible capital, which is disproportionately large in rich countries. (The average American has 12 times the intangible capital of the average Mexican but just three times the natural and produced capital.) The majority of the value, it found, is explained by the rule-of-law index. Furthermore, it determined that "the correlation between generalized trust and rule of law is high," meaning those two factors tend to go together. Trust between people in a society and adherence to the rule of law both flow from the nation's spiritual capital, and almost half a country's total wealth can be attributed to these factors![36]

Living Off the Trust Fund

Spiritual capital accounts are slow to build, but once grown, they're also slow to deplete. That's the situation we're encountering in the United States, where the nation's spiritual capital account has been built up over many years. But I believe we're now slowly drawing down on that accumulated capital. As the West moves from a moral environment to an amoral environment, spiritual capital is being reduced, and in some places even exhausted.

Even in nations that enjoy large spiritual capital reserves, there are pockets where biblical principles are generally foreign to the market. For example, used car salesmen are often considered the least honest in Gallup's annual poll of occupations. Now there are certainly some good used car dealers. But while there are exceptions, most transactions in this market are amoral at best. Dishonest dealings and shenanigans are all too common. You never know if you're being sold a lemon, and if you're like most people, you've lost any expectations that the dealer will reveal what's wrong with the car. He's not serving you; he's in it for himself. So you'll want to have your own mechanic, someone you can trust, take a look at the vehicle. There's also plenty of bargaining in the process. How much can the dealer get out of you? Perhaps he can gouge someone who's not really aware of the car's value. Perhaps he can fast-talk you into paying more than you should. The entire experience is adversarial and sickening.

Contrast that with what the experience would be like in a moral environment, one in which the other party is committed to doing what's right in the eyes of God. What if you could have complete trust in the seller—and he in you? (Think about what this transaction might look like if you were buying the car from your father or brother or someone else you could trust to act in your interest.) You'd trust him to inform you of the car's known problems. He might trust you to test-drive it for a day. You'd trust him to quote you a fair price. He might trust you to pay it off on an installment plan—with no credit check or collateral. How much more pleasant that exchange is than the nightmare many experience with used car dealers today!

"Those who believe that you can be successful in business without faith are of course right," states Dr. Malloch. "You can be successful in any sphere, provided you have luck, skill, and trust in your own powers. But often you will be drawing on spiritual capital that has been built up by others, and which is stored in the virtues of a workforce or the customs of a market."[37] Business that profits by cutting corners and operating dishonestly does so because there's a general trust in the market, a healthy spiritual capital reserve. But it also reduces that reserve in the process.

The Culture Barrier to Growing Spiritual Capital

If the West is living off spiritual capital that's been accumulated over many decades and is largely institutionalized in the customs of the market, the situation is far different in most developing nations. Not only are they starting with a low spiritual capital reserve, but their cultures do not lend themselves to growing the account. The predominant attitudes, values, and beliefs can have very deep roots that sometimes constitute a barrier to building spiritual capital.

Even when a country has experienced spiritual transformation, if that newfound faith does not translate into a renewed marketplace, there is no spiritual capital growth. If the marketplace is to be redeemed and the spiritual capital account is to be grown, godly character, biblical practices, and fruit of the Spirit must permeate the nation's business practices. Guatemala has seen a recent move of the Spirit, and today half the country considers itself evangelical Christian.[38] One might assume that with the worship of God would come an economic transformation, but the country's development is stagnating.

When I was there in the fall of 2004, the reasons became apparent: The country's business environment is still dominated by amoral practices, perhaps the most glaring of which is *caveat emptor*—let the buyer beware. In Guatemala, the burden is on the buyer to ensure the deal is good. If a product or service proves poor or defective, or if it turns out the buyer was taken, the fault rests with the buyer, not with the seller.

In Scripture, God instructs the nation of Israel, and all of us, to deal honestly in business by setting forth the following law: "Do not have two differing weights in your bag—one heavy, one light. Do not have two differing measures in your house—one large, one small. You must have accurate and honest weights and measures, so that you may live long in the land the Lord your God is giving you. For the Lord your God detests anyone who does these things, anyone who deals dishonestly" (Deut. 25:13–16).

I spoke to an audience of Guatemalan business leaders and politicians about the concept of spiritual capital and explained that the practice of *caveat emptor* must be changed if their nation is to experience any economic blessing. I was told I'd hit the nail on the head. This unbiblical buyer-beware practice is thoroughly ingrained, but if it's not reformed, the Guatemalan economy will continue to stagnate. God will not bless sin. The Bible is very clear on this point.

Building Spiritual Capital and Transforming a Nation

So the question is how a country like Guatemala that has very little spiritual capital starts to build its reserve and head down the path toward economic blessings. How do biblical values become pervasive in the marketplace? It may take less than you think. Consider the story of two grocers who changed a nation's business culture.

It was the Middle Ages in London; dishonest scales and measures in commerce were commonplace. Two merchants were convinced this ran contrary to biblical teaching: "The Lord abhors dishonest scales, but accurate weights are his delight" (Prov. 11:1). So these merchants resolved to align their business practices with their faith. They agreed to be mutually accountable to each other for honest weights and measures. Each would test the other's scales and verify their accuracy.

It was highly uncertain that their pact to keep each other accountable to true weights and measures would yield economic benefits. Indeed, it probably seemed they were jeopardizing their chances for success. These two merchants were in a very competitive market, and they wouldn't be able to match the perceived low prices of their dishonest competitors. But they were committed to following God's commands regardless of the outcome.

The decision to use honest weights and measures was not a simple or easy one. Just imagine how difficult it must have been. Imagine all the grocers in the London market with signs offering apples for a penny a pound while two guys are offering apples for perhaps 1.2 pennies a pound. There was almost an expectation on behalf of buyers that they would be sold short, so people might easily think these two guys were not only cheating them but gouging them to boot! And it wasn't like these guys were well financed. In those days, merchants lived day to day. No sales that day meant no income. And if they couldn't pay their bills, they were imprisoned. (There was no Social Security safety net.) So the decision to follow God's laws and the promptings of the Holy Spirit could have serious negative consequences—certainly greater than today.

As it became known that these grocers were honest in their dealings, business flowed their way. Other merchants took notice, and soon they wanted to join those who operated on biblical values. Businessmen in other trades also took notice and set up ethical standards and performance values of their own.

So were born the Livery Companies, trade organizations that unite workers in various occupations and hold them to high standards. In the fourteenth century, King Edward III granted charters to the original 12 Great Companies, which included the grocers, mercers, drapers, fishmongers, and goldsmiths.

The Livery Companies were very much driven by religious conviction. They were closely linked to the Church, and prayerful worship typically preceded meetings. The fact that they were motivated by deep faith was also evident in their names, such as "The Most Worshipful Company of Goldsmiths" and mottos, such as "In God is all our hope" (plumbers) and "Praise God for all" (bakers). (Appendix C contains images of some of the Livery Companies' seals. The mottos in the crests reflect the deep religious commitment of those in the organizations.) Based on biblical principles, the tenets of the Livery Companies prescribed ethical practices and specified strict penalties for those who violated the trust. The term "baker's dozen" originated from the Worshipful Company of Bakers' practice of going beyond the customer's expectations and including more bread as insurance against shortchanging him.

Customers rewarded businesses that subjected themselves to the biblical values of the Livery Companies with their trust, loyalty, and satisfaction. In due time, virtually every trade had established a set of ethical and performance standards, and membership in a Livery Company became essential to business success. Along with their members, the trade associations prospered and funded schools and charitable arms. The Liveries became such a central part of London life and government that by the fifteenth century they elected the city's mayors and sheriffs from among their ranks.

Livery Companies have continued through the centuries, currently numbering more than one hundred. Today's organizations are more committed to charity and faith-based good works than to reinforcing ethical and competent business. But that doesn't diminish their central role in London's economic growth, both in medieval times and beyond. Two grocers stepped out in faith and in the process transformed the business climate to one that operated on biblical principles and grew spiritual capital. And they set the marketplace on a path to economic blessings.[39]

London's transition from an immoral business environment to one that grew spiritual capital had a number of add-on effects. Consider that London became the financial capital of the world for many centuries. It spawned the concept of political freedom and important Christian political thinkers such as Thomas Hobbes. American freedom and independence came from thinking and the concept of capitalism developed by Adam Smith, himself influenced by watching how the system worked in London. And by the 19th century, London was the hub of the modern missions movement to Africa, India, and China.

The Spiritual Aspect of Spiritual Capital

We've described spiritual capital in economic and "non-spiritual" terms, noting that it grows trust, lowers transaction costs, and thus leads to greater economic development and prosperity. But is there a spiritual aspect to spiritual capital? Absolutely. It has to do with God's desire to bring life and supernatural blessing to the marketplace.

Wherever the Spirit of God is, there is life. Because we are followers of Jesus, the Spirit of God lives in us. And wherever we are, including the marketplace, there is life, as long as we allow the Spirit of God to partner in our work. It doesn't take everyone in a company or industry to be committed followers of Jesus for this principle to apply. Consider the effect of the two grocers in medieval London who believed and put their faith to work in the marketplace. They ultimately brought life to an entire economy.

God also begins to bless beyond what we consider normal. He blesses in a way that would be considered "supernatural." In the final chapter, I'll tell the story of Almolonga, a town in Central America that has seen a complete spiritual turnaround and is now experiencing economic blessings that can only be described as supernatural. Their previously unremarkable land has been transformed, and it's now claimed to be forty times more productive than any other place on earth, including the valleys next door. I have seen both the crop output and the area where it's grown, and I can believe the claim! The vegetables produced there are not only numerous but also enormous—the biggest you'll ever see and yet the most delicious I've ever experienced. They are an amazing testimony to God.

Yes, the economics of spiritual capital bring a stable and improved environment for economic development—but spiritual capital is much, much more. It includes the Master's hand as a partner in our work to bring life and do the supernatural. I'm convinced these supernatural experiences are heaven's "normal." When we allow the Creator of life to partner with us, we can expect miracles to happen. We can expect spiritual capital to bring prosperity and glory to God.

In secular business schools, you will find little or no appreciation for what has been the "secret sauce" of successful commerce in our country—the accumulation of spiritual capital through faith in action in the marketplace. Few people or institutions today appreciate the value generated when followers of Jesus bring biblical principles and the fruit of the Spirit to their business and build spiritual capital. A clear understanding of the relationship between honoring God and achieving economic success helps us bridge the divide between faith and work and integrate the two.

Leaving Business School

The tools of the trade taught at business school are helpful, but they fail to consider a higher purpose for capitalism than self-interest and profit. They fail to identify the foundation of successful business—biblical values and a culture of trust. They fail to demand moral attitudes and actions beyond what's required by the legal code.

It took me decades to discover some of the truths that I didn't learn in business school, truths that helped me integrate faith and work:

- While profit is a necessary by-product of serving others, it cannot be the overriding objective of business. The real goal of business is not to maximize profits or shareholder value—it's to serve others to the glory of God.
- Good business principles such as integrity, honesty, trust, service, and fairness are in fact biblical principles. Thus, successful business people who operate on biblical principles are not successful despite following them; they are successful because they follow them.
- Spiritual capital produces the faith, trust, and commitment that others will do what is right in the eyes of God. It is the unrecognized pillar of capitalism, the essential oil that makes an economic system run.

What we have culled from our business training contributes to our compartmentalized life, but there's much more that reinforces our segregation of faith and work. And unfortunately, those additional barriers to an integrated life come from church.

PART III

What I Didn't
Learn in Church

How many times have you heard the phrase "(s)he's in full-time ministry"? Isn't it always applied to those who work for a religious outfit—a church, a mission, a parachurch organization? Many Christians in the marketplace are left with the impression that what they spend most of their waking weekday hours doing is at best of no interest to God and at worst a curse God has imposed on mankind.

The church often fails to identify or affirm spiritual value in our everyday work. Thus, we perceive the nature of our work, the goal of our work, and the outcome of our work as lacking spiritual significance. We conclude that secular business and a sincere desire to serve God are mutually exclusive. And so the compartmentalized life is reinforced—by messages from the church.

In this Part, we will address several misconceptions often found and taught in the church. Does God frown on profit and wealth? (Chapter 7) What is ministry and what is work—and are some types of work a higher calling than others? (Chapter 8) And what is the proper role of the church with regard to those in the marketplace? (Chapter 9) Let's see if we can't develop a better understanding of the biblical paradigm for work and business that is often not found in church.

CHAPTER 7

Profit & Wealth— The Great Bugaboos!

Managers must convert society's needs into opportunities for profitable business.
> (Dr. Peter F. Drucker, writer on management)

To allow wealth creation legitimacy is not to endow it with autonomy.
> (Lord Brian Griffiths, Vice Chairman, Goldman Sachs)

Democratic capitalism is neither the Kingdom of God nor without sin. Yet all other known systems of political economy are worse.
> (Michael Novak, philosopher and diplomat)

The Divide

"I'm flabbergasted," says Jack Feldballe, founder of Renaissance Video, "by the degree of abnormal criticism and suspicion of wealth you see among clergy of all faiths. They think that because an individual is wealthy it was ill-gotten gain at someone else's expense."[40] That's a tough assessment, but I'm afraid my experience echoes his. I have noticed a prevailing attitude in the church that wealth is evil and that those who make a profit are taking advantage of their fellow man. And even when well-meaning church leaders do not espouse this belief, the notion is often inferred or presumed as a result of silence on the topic from the pulpit.

The perceived church attitude toward profit and wealth is another point that reinforces the compartmentalized life. We are taught the spiritual ideal is unencumbered poverty and charity. Business, on the other hand, requires material resources and profit. It's unsettling to be faced with the prospect that God looks unfavorably on both of these. No wonder many are left feeling guilty and questioning whether there's an irreconcilable divide between their faith and their work!

But what I didn't learn in church is that wealth and profit are not inherently evil—nor are they the necessary evidence of personal righteousness. God doesn't judge us by the degree of our profit and wealth; he's concerned about our attitude toward them and our stewardship of them.

Profit: Is It Morally Wrong?

Several years ago, I gave a seminar on how to start a business. It was a three-day conference in a Swedish church. More than a thousand Christians attended. At the conclusion of the first segment, several approached me to question a basic premise. How could I as a Christian justify starting a for-profit business venture?

Unsure of the reason for their objections, I sought to know what they thought of large established companies like Ikea or Volvo. "We have no problem with them," they replied. "They provide our people employment and pensions." What then was the objection to entrepreneurship?

After further discussion it became apparent that their discomfort was really with profit objectives. It didn't mesh with their theology and sense of justice. Without direct input from their church or pastor, they assumed the socialist attitude of their culture must be biblically correct. I had to revise my next two days to teach on the role of profit and wealth.

Many in the church have concluded likewise that profit runs contrary to a spirit of love and service. How can anyone in good conscience make a profit off someone else? Aren't nonprofit organizations inherently nobler than for-profit ventures?

Both nonprofit and for-profit organizations should focus on using gifts and resources for the glory of God. Most nonprofits are indeed engaged in commendable work that benefits society, but it is their mission rather than the absence of a profit that should earn them praise. Many for-profit organizations offer useful services as well. In fact, the greater the benefit of the product or service to the recipient, the greater the potential for profit. So don't think your work would have more meaning if it were conducted in a nonprofit setting. There is no direct correlation between an absence of profit and benefit to society.

In many parables, while making a spiritual application, Jesus affirmed the right to earn a profit. In the parable of the talents (Matt. 25:14–30), a nobleman going on a journey entrusted three servants with money. Two earned a 100 percent return while he was gone, but the third simply hid the money and showed no profit. That third servant was severely rebuked for failing to earn a return. A profit was expected. In another story, the parable of the tenants (Luke 20:9–16), a man who'd rented his vineyard to some farmers sent his servant to collect a portion of the proceeds. He was entitled to a share of the profits, but all attempts to collect the lease failed. So a nobleman could expect a multiplication of investment monies, a landowner could expect lease payments—these are returns on assets, or profits, that Jesus was affirming!

Sadly, many in the church have adopted the tenet of socialism that aggregate wealth is constant. Thus, if one person's making a profit, it must come at another's expense. But the total economic pie is not fixed, as socialists would suggest. Successful commerce means that goods and services are created, aggregate wealth grows, and the standard of living increases. There are certainly examples of ill-gotten wealth, and those activities that rob the nation of spiritual capital cannot be justified. But when businesses that truly serve others earn a profit, it should not diminish the nobility of their work. In fact, in a competitive world, profits can be viewed as the sign that others are being served in a way that creates an aggregate benefit and grows aggregate wealth.

When discussing profits in Chapter 4, we noted that while profits are not the goal of business, they are necessary for business to survive and grow. As Peter Drucker said, "Profit is not the explanation, cause, or rationale of business behavior and business decisions, but rather the test of their validity. If archangels instead of businessmen sat in directors' chairs, they would still have to be concerned with profitability, despite their total lack of personal interest in making profits."[41] I have seen a number of well-meaning businessmen attempt to run businesses without a profit. To my knowledge, none have succeeded. Without profit, a business cannot continue to serve people to the glory of God.

Money: Is It the Root of All Evil?

Wealth and profit are sometimes such bugaboos because there's a belief that money is the root of all evil. That's certainly enough to cause fear and anxiety around the subject! Better to keep away, some conclude, lest it lead us down a wrong path.

There are indeed temptations to worship money above God. The Apostle Paul warns us, "The love of money is a root of all kinds of evil. Some people, eager for money, have wandered from the faith and pierced themselves with many griefs" (1 Tim. 6:10). Note first that it's the *love* of money rather than *money itself* that's called the source of various evils. Money and wealth are not inherently wrong. They are neutral resources that can be used for noble purposes or for ignoble purposes. And second, a lack of earthly riches does not make one immune to the love of money. The poor can idolize money just as much as the wealthy. The critical point is our attitude toward money.

Another view found in the church considers those who are affluent to be less spiritual—perhaps not even true followers of Jesus. Didn't Jesus say that the rich couldn't inherit the kingdom of God? Let's examine that passage (Matt. 19:16–24). One day a rich young ruler came to Jesus and asked what he must do to possess eternal life.

"Obey the commandments," was the reply. Jesus went on to list six specific commandments.

Apparently this rich young man had kept these since his childhood, and he inquired, "What do I still lack?"

Jesus responded, "If you want to be perfect, go, sell your possessions and give to the poor, and you will have treasure in heaven. Then come, follow me." The young man walked away sad, we are told, because he had great wealth. "I tell you the truth," Jesus said to his disciples, "it is hard for a rich man to enter the kingdom of heaven. Again I tell you, it is easier for a camel to go through the eye of a needle than for a rich man to enter the kingdom of God."

You may have discerned that Jesus wasn't really denouncing wealth by instructing the young man to rid himself of his plentiful possessions. Instead, he was getting at the man's heart—what he truly valued. The ultimate revelation was that the young man's material possessions were an idol that kept him from following Jesus.

Many who read this passage envision a large mammal and a small sewing needle and conclude that those with wealth don't stand a chance. What's translated "eye of a needle" refers to the trade entrance in the city wall through which camels packed with merchandise would enter. It was a narrow passageway, and when the load was too large, some of it would need to be removed. This sheds light on Jesus' statement. Wealth can keep us from entering the City of God if we're not willing to part with it—if it's got our heart. That was the case with the rich young ruler he'd just encountered.

R. G. LeTourneau was an American businessman in the first half of the 20th century whose attitude toward wealth exemplified Jesus' teaching. With no more than an eighth-grade education, LeTourneau overcame early setbacks and failures to become a prolific inventor responsible for nearly 300 patents. He parlayed a novel bulldozer into an enormous company that produced some of the world's largest machinery, from earthmovers to bridge builders to portable offshore drilling rigs. Nearly 70 percent of the earthmoving equipment used during World War II was LeTourneau's machinery. As you might imagine, this business proved profitable, and he was greatly blessed financially.

While R.G. LeTourneau had money, money didn't have him. He gave ninety percent of his income to Christian work and lived off the other ten percent, a practice he continued even when his company was in financial jeopardy. He found that as he did this, God blessed him even more. "I shovel out the money, and God shovels it back to me—but God has a bigger shovel," the earthmoving industrialist explained. Though he worked hard to give away the money God had given him, he still had $90 million when he died in 1969, an amount equivalent to more than $500 million today. It is my understanding he instructed his heirs to give the rest away in the next ten years following his death. "The question is not how much of my money I give to God, but rather how much of God's money I keep for myself," LeTourneau said.[42]

Toward a Biblical View of Prosperity

The "Poverty" Gospel

I have found that many sincere believers feel that wealth is the evil enemy of a righteous life and that poverty is somehow a more desirable and spiritual state to which one should aspire. Didn't Jesus state that the poor are blessed? Poverty holds a certain romantic appeal to those who envision a life free from all the earthly trappings of material possessions. One special characteristic of the order founded by St. Francis of Assisi is a vow of poverty. Indeed, a trait we admire about pastors and missionaries is their humble salary and lowly lifestyle. It must be a component of truly serving God, we conclude.

But the Scriptures don't reflect that romantic view of poverty. A number of Proverbs warn against habits that lead to poverty. The poor are certainly not considered more favored, and if you've ever seen real poverty, you understand why. Those who have inadequate shelter and go hungry for days would hardly describe their state as "blessed." They certainly wouldn't subscribe to a romantic view of poverty. God "delights in the well-being of his servant" (Ps. 35:27) and promises a multitude of economic blessings to those who obey him and follow his commands (Deut. 28:1–14).

The "Prosperity" Gospel

Some in the church have taken the notion of God's blessing on the righteous to conclude that he will necessarily bestow great material possessions and physical health on his people. The "prosperity gospel" posits that health and wealth are the evidence of right standing with God. Sickness and poverty are thus seen as evidence of sin or insufficient faith.

It is difficult to sustain this theology from examples in Scripture. Sometimes God uses difficulty to teach us and perfect us (James 1:2–3). Job is described as a "blameless and upright man" who "feared God and shunned evil" (Job 1:1). Though Job was righteous, God allowed Satan to throw him into poverty and subject him to sickness. There are plenty of other examples in Scripture where God's faithful people do not experience prosperity as the world might define it. Perhaps the most notable example is the life of Jesus. So this opposite extreme to the "poverty gospel" also falls short.

God's Prosperity

Having described two theologies that miss the mark of the rich biblical teaching about wealth and profit, the poverty gospel and the prosperity gospel, I should briefly outline several points Scripture *does* make about prosperity.

- *Wealth is to be in all areas.* Rather than material wealth, being "rich toward God" should be the goal (Luke 12:21). When God granted Solomon a wish, he asked for wisdom to discern between right and wrong. His request was for spiritual wealth, and God further blessed him with material and physical wealth to carry out his work (1 Kings 3:11–14). God wants his people to recognize his blessings in all areas.
- *Wealth is from God.* Jesus taught that good gifts come from our Father in heaven (Matt. 7:11). It is tempting to believe that financial gains in business result from our own wisdom, strategy, and execution. But even those talents come from God! "Remember the Lord your God, for it is he who gives you the ability to produce wealth" (Deut. 8:18). We need to remember that

it is God who gives all good things, including material wealth.

- *Wealth is to be managed.* God has entrusted us with resources, some little and some much, and as we glean from the parable of the talents, he holds us accountable for wise deployment of these resources. "Possession and direction of the forces of wealth are as legitimate an expression of the redemptive rule of God in human life as is Bible teaching or a prayer meeting," notes theologian Dallas Willard.[43] Stewardship is a significant responsibility and ministry, and we should embrace our role as stewards.

- *Wealth is to be used for God's purpose.* Money is neither inherently good nor inherently bad, but the purposes for which it's deployed can run the gamut. As stewards of God's resources, we should ensure that it's used for his purposes, and tithing is an important part of that. Paul instructs those who are rich that they should be ready to give, willing to share, and generous on every occasion (1 Tim. 6:17–18; 2 Cor. 9:9–15). And God promises to further bless those who are faithful in this way: "Bring the whole tithe into the storehouse ... and see if I will not throw open the floodgates of heaven and pour out so much blessing that you will not have room enough for it" (Mal. 3:10).

- *Wealth is not our source of trust.* Paul instructed Timothy about the dangers of relying on wealth: "Command those who are rich in this present world not to be arrogant nor to put their hope in wealth, which is so uncertain, but to put their hope in God" (1 Tim. 6:17). Scripture tells us that "wealth is worthless in the day of wrath, but righteousness delivers from death" (Prov. 11:4). Neither riches nor poverty makes us any more deserving. God considers the heart. We are saved by the personal righteousness available through Jesus.

- *Wealth is to be enjoyed.* Many followers of Jesus are moved by the economic disparity found in the world, and conditions in many regions are troubling to the church. Guilt and an embarrassment of riches prevent some from enjoying what God has bestowed. While we are to realize that wealth has a kingdom purpose, God also wants us to enjoy it! Scripture says, God "richly provides us with everything for our enjoyment" (1 Tim. 6:17). But that doesn't afford us limitless latitude to indulge and abdicate our stewardship responsibilities. We should each seek God's guidance on the defining line.

Bridging the Divide

How can the believing businessperson reconcile his economic requirement of profit and resulting financial gain with the notion that God frowns on profit and wealth? At a minimum, we're left with a deep disconnect between our work and our faith. And many of us have dealt with this seemingly irreconcilable divide by compartmentalizing our faith from our work.

We've now covered two relevant milestones on the road to bridging the divide between business's singular focus on profits and the church's critical attitude toward profit and wealth. The first, in Chapter 4, is the recognition that, contrary to what we learned in business school, the goal of business is not profit-maximization. The real goal of business is to serve others to the glory of God. The second milestone, in this chapter, is the understanding that, contrary to the prevailing attitude in parts of the church, profit and wealth are not inherently evil. Profit is a necessary sign that others are being served effectively, and we should not feel guilt or shame when God entrusts us with financial resources.

There is another area in which I've found attitudes in the church contribute to work–faith compartmentalization. And this misconception affects our perception of and attitude toward our daily work. Is it really a curse we must endure, or does our work actually have spiritual value? Does God consider business spiritually inferior to "full-time Christian work"? Could our secular work even be a ministry and a calling? We'll turn to that next.

CHAPTER 8

The Spiritual Role of Work and Business

In every letter St. Paul wrote he demonstrated that a Christian's work is a natural, inevitable and faithful development out of God's work.

(Dr. Eugene Peterson, author and theologian)

The truth of calling means that for followers of Christ, everyone, everywhere, and in everything lives the whole of life as a response to God's call. Yet, this holistic character of calling has often been distorted to become a form of dualism that elevates the spiritual at the expense of the secular.

(Dr. Os Guinness, writer and social critic)

The "layman" need never think of his humbler task as being inferior to that of his minister. Let every man abide in the calling wherein he is called and his work will be as sacred as the work of the ministry. It is not what a man does that determines whether his work is sacred or secular, it is why he does it. The motive is everything.

(A. W. Tozer, author and pastor)

How We View Work

How often have you gotten to the end of a tough week and thought, "Thank God it's Friday!"? The workplace sure can be a source of frustration, difficulty, and stress. Moreover, it takes from our leisure time and commitments to family and God. Isn't toil a result of the curse God put on mankind after the fall of Adam and Eve? It sure seems that way to many of us. And shouldn't we be doing something more meaningful with our lives than working toward promotions and increasing our companies' stock prices?

Most of us have no choice. We've got to earn a living, so we do our time. As the popular bumper sticker says, "I owe, I owe, so off to work I go." Not a particularly noble or enthusiastic view of work, but it's one many in the workplace share. When we lack purpose and fulfillment in our work, it becomes "just a job." I have found many people are resigned to this situation, whether they are followers of Jesus or not.

Without conviction about any intrinsic value to our work, we're often resigned to the fact that day-to-day work will be unfulfilling. Many of us are saddled with the notion that work is a curse, the result of original sin. Or at best, it's considered a necessary evil that keeps us from more important matters, such as serving God. We may long to invest ourselves in something that's more redeeming—perhaps something with a higher ministry component. So the belief that our work in the marketplace lacks intrinsic and spiritual value most certainly creates a barrier to an integrated life!

What I didn't learn in church is that work is good, mandated, and sacred, that business is not spiritually inferior to work in a Christian organization, and that our everyday work can be both a ministry and a high calling. God cares deeply about our work. If we are to break down the walls of compartmentalization between work and faith, we need to recognize the spiritual value of our work. So let me lay out this paradigm of work. The following truths will transform your perception of and attitude toward your daily business.

The Spiritual Value of Work

What Is Work?

Perhaps the best place to start is by defining the term *work*. What does it entail? John Stott puts it nicely when he says that "work is the expenditure of energy (whether manual or mental or both) in the service of others, which brings fulfillment to the worker, benefit to the community and glory to God."[44] Work is serving others.

Those of us in the business world are engaged in work, as are those in the broader marketplace, be they professors, pastors, or politicians. But expending energy to serve others need not include financial compensation. Students, volunteers, and homemakers are all engaged in valuable work as well. Whether there is an element of compensation involved or not, work is service to others done to the glory of God.

A God Who Works

Those of us who spend a large portion of our lives working can take comfort in the fact that God holds a very high view of work. Indeed, God is a worker himself. The entire first chapter of the Bible is an account of his workweek. He spent six days exerting himself in creating the universe, and on the seventh he rested. Since that first week, God has been actively working throughout history to uphold creation, meet the broad needs of his many creatures, and work out his purposes.[45]

Jesus said, "My Father is always at his work to this very day, and I, too, am working" (John 5:17). Though Scripture focuses on his three years working as an itinerant preacher,

Jesus spent considerably more time working as a carpenter. Like many of us, he was identified by his profession. "Isn't this the carpenter?" the people of Nazareth asked when they first heard him preach (Mark 6:3). As the oldest child, he probably would have taken over the family's carpentry business, managing siblings and other family members. He would have faced a number of the same work challenges business people encounter today: serving customers, paying suppliers, managing workers, ensuring quality, and earning a profit. So our first clue that God esteems work is that he engages in it himself.

Work Is Good

When God finished his six days of creating, he looked upon his work and called it very good. Then he called Adam and Eve to continue his work by naming the animals, developing the land, and taking care of his creation. And the work they did was good, for sin had not yet entered the world.

When Adam sinned, work was affected in some profound ways. It became difficult and painful. Because of his disobedience, Adam was told the ground would be cursed, that it would produce thorns and thistles, and that harvesting food from the land would now involve painful, sweaty toil (Gen. 3:17–19). Sin also imparted a degree of futility to our work, meaning that our work will never find completion. In a fallen world that tends toward disorder and disintegration, there will always be more to do.[46] But while the first sin introduced pain and frustration to work, it didn't change God's analysis that work is inherently good. And God made no distinction between sacred and secular work.

Created, Mandated, and Gifted to Work

We are told that God created humans in his own image. An important aspect of that is making man a fellow worker.

Adam was commanded to tend and keep the garden of Eden. Like him, we are created in God's image as a worker. "We are God's workmanship, created in Christ Jesus to do good works, which God prepared in advance for us to do" (Eph. 2:10). We are created to work, to do good work.

We're also mandated to work. Paul encourages us to work with our hands so that we do not become a burden to others (1 Thess. 4:11–12), and he warns against idleness (2 Thess. 3:6–15). We should work as unto God (Eph. 6:5–9), and everything we do should be to his glory (1 Cor. 10:31). In doing so, we are doing good work.

God not only commands us to work, but he imparts to us the skills to deploy in the process. "It is he who gives you the ability to produce wealth," we're told (Deut. 8:18). In short, we are created to work, mandated to work, and gifted to work.

Contributing to God's Work

We are created to work, but not in pursuit of our own fancy. We are to be co-workers with God, promoting his agenda and furthering his work in the world. "All legitimate work is an extension of God's work," state Doug Sherman and William Hendricks.[47] Legitimate work is activity that somehow promotes his purposes in the world and doesn't promote the opposite.

"Okay," you say, "I work in the secular marketplace, and I'm unclear on the spiritual value of my work." If that's your realization, take heart. You're certainly not alone. I find that many people have difficulty articulating the spiritual value of their daily work. Sure, we can identify how a missionary or a pastor advances God's goals in the world, but what about a marketer, an accountant, or a software engineer? Sometimes the way our work contributes to God's work is not so obvious.

I'm reminded of the old story of some laborers working on a building project. A curious traveler approached one of them and asked what they were doing. "We're laying stone," the worker responded without looking up. After glancing around a bit, the observer asked another man the same question. Pointing to a developing structure, he replied, "We're making a wall." The observer moved on to another worker and posed the question a third time. With joy on his face and pride in his work, he exclaimed, "We're building a cathedral to the glory of God!"

Many of us need to see our work through the larger picture of God's plans in order to identify how our work is really the construction of a cathedral. That may be a difficult realization, especially if we're operating with the mind-set that God's only concerned with religious matters.

My friend Dave Seeba is a Certified Public Accountant (CPA). On the surface, Dave's office would seem like a typical accountancy with CPAs and professionals at various levels working on a variety of accounting projects: individual and business tax returns, estate tax planning, audits, and consulting on accounting organization. Nothing terribly spiritual, exciting, or redeeming about number crunching, you might think. Yet Dave most certainly views his job as building a cathedral, and his work reflects that reality.

Dave considers his true mission as an advisor to help people use their money for the purposes God has laid on their hearts. Many of his clients are Christians in Silicon Valley who suddenly find themselves blessed with personal assets. Dave understands that wealth comes with responsibilities. In order to best help his clients accomplish their philanthropic objectives while blessing their families in effective ways, Dave has sought to develop expertise in a number of disciplines. I've seen him interact with legal counsel and often prove himself more aware of laws and proper procedures than those in that field. He keeps up with ever-changing tax regulations and techniques, and he often calls his clients with new ideas to help them manage their money and give more effectively.

Rather than view his job as completing one tax return after another ("laying stone") or saving clients as much as possible in taxes ("making a wall"), Dave sees his work as assisting others in maximizing resources for God's kingdom ("building a cathedral"). That's his mission, his way of contributing to God's work.

Do you see your job as just laying stone? If we are to live abundant business lives, we need to appreciate how our work is really the construction of a cathedral. We must recognize how we can contribute to God's purposes in the marketplace. We need to understand how our work can be a ministry and a high calling.

Called to Business

There is a widespread belief that calling, like ministry, pertains only to church-related work. The term "calling" is used loosely in the church to mean a number of things, but it almost always refers to serving a church or parachurch ministry in an occupational or voluntary capacity. "Calling" is a spiritual term reserved for those pursuing noble and sacrificial work, we're led to believe, and business doesn't seem to fill the bill.

In fact, everyone has a personal call that is manifested through personal discipleship, personal experience, personal gifting, and personal desire. "While it is extraordinary for people to have a direct, verbal 'call' (as in Acts 16:9–10)," notes theologian Paul Stevens, "it is entirely ordinary for God to create a desire in our hearts to do the very thing needed, whether in the church or in the world. Business people are called in this sense, as are engineers, homemakers, craftspersons, pastors, and missionaries."[48] Many of us are called to minister in the business world, just as others are called to minister in the church. "In making shoes, the cobbler serves God, obeys his calling from God, quite as much as the preacher of the Word," notes Martin Luther.[49] They're both called to their work.

A Higher Calling

So we can be called to secular work. But everything we've been taught explicitly or implicitly leads us to believe a preacher's calling must be higher than a cobbler's. Today many parts of the Christian church operate under a de facto caste system that elevates the calling and nobility of work "in ministry" above that of "secular" occupations. Accountants, salespeople, lawyers, and factory workers aren't engaged in bad work, many Christians believe, but there's nothing spiritually significant to their work either. The assumption, perhaps unstated, is that they're pursuing worldly success and worldly rewards rather than serving God with their work. It's no wonder we perceive a lack of spiritual value in our work and conclude that we need to enter the ministry to really serve God!

But are there higher callings, and what really does constitute the highest personal calling in God's economy? In short, there is no universal highest personal calling. We all have different gifts. Some people are gifted at making shoes, others at preaching the Word. God's personal calling to an individual is in harmony with his gifting. It's that which incorporates God's unique design, gifting, and direction, and it will vary from person to person. However or wherever you're called to serve, that's your highest personal calling.

"The official Church wastes time and energy, and moreover, commits sacrilege, in demanding that secular workers should neglect their proper vocation in order to do Christian work—by which [the Church] means ecclesiastical work," declares Dorothy Sayers.[50] I've seen too many fall prey to the notion that in order to serve God in their work they must pursue some "higher calling to full-time Christian work," irrespective of the passions, talents, and training God has bestowed. The result is almost always disastrous.

I have been in communication recently with a gifted young man, a committed believer with a heart for God. After earning a degree in mechanical engineering from M.I.T., he enrolled in business school. During his first year, he became a follower of Jesus and developed a desire to serve him. He'd "learned" that he needed to forsake business in order to truly serve God. So, as this young man was completing his business school education, he decided to become a missionary. He joined a mission agency after graduation and spent three years in the Philippines.

But that experience proved far from the joy he associated with serving God. During his time as an overseas missionary, he explained to me, he was completely broken. The work didn't correspond to his gifting or passion. He was miserable. Upon returning to the United States, he took a job as a consultant. He's currently trying to determine where God wants him, but this much he now knows: His calling is to business. He has come to see that business is not a calling that is spiritually inferior to overseas missionary work. It can be a noble and high calling. In fact, for him it's the highest calling.

We're All Priests

We need to understand another important truth: all Christians are priests. That includes every believer—the minister, the mother, and the manager. In the Old Testament, the majority of God's people were considered unclean and excluded from the priesthood. Not so in the New Testament, as the work of Jesus made all believers holy and priests. "You ...

are being built into a spiritual house to be a holy priesthood," Peter tells us. "You are a chosen people, a royal priesthood, a holy nation, a people belonging to God" (1 Pet. 2:5, 9). The book of Revelation tells us that Jesus "made us to be a kingdom and priests to serve his God and Father" (Rev. 1:6).

It was Martin Luther who rejected the prevalent division of the church into a holy clergy and a mundane laity. "Monks and clergy, Luther realized, were no more valued in God's economy than anyone else. In fact, all believers have a 'priestly calling' in whatever roles they undertake."[51] Though the church has often perpetuated the dualistic clergy–laity division, in God's economy there really aren't two classes of believers—there's only one. We are all holy priests. Think about that for a moment. What are the implications for your responsibility to the workplace and the value of your work? It means that we're called to do important ministry.

The Ministry of Business

The common phrase "full-time ministry" that's applied to those in church-related work implies that the rest of us aren't engaged in "full-time" ministry during our work hours, but that's patently false. All followers of Jesus are called to be in full-time ministry, whether they're employed by a church, a company, or another organization. This is an important point at the heart of the paradigm shift many of us need: Our work in business *is* ministry. Let that sink in, because it goes far to break down the compartmentalization of work life and spiritual life.

Why has God placed his followers in the business world? I suspect the majority of believers would immediately think of the opportunities and responsibilities to share their faith with those around them at work. God has certainly put his people in positions where they can introduce others to him (our ministry *at* work), but his desires go further. He also cares deeply about our ministry *of* work and our ministry *to* work. Let me explain the threefold ministry of our work life.[52]

1. The Ministry at Work

Most followers of Jesus see the ministry value of their jobs in providing a place where they can demonstrate love and share their faith. We have an opportunity to touch the people we encounter in the workplace—engaging in conversation over lunch or in the hallway, displaying evidence of faith in one's office, or inviting co-workers to a Bible study. It's our ministry <u>at</u> work.

As CEO of Inmac, I wanted partners, customers, employees, and visitors to know that my personal faith affected the way people were treated and business was conducted at the company. Perhaps more important, I wanted them to know that God desired to have a personal relationship with them, too. So I placed spiritual and Bible tracts in our company's lobby with an accompanying letter:

> ABOUT THESE PAMPHLETS
>
> *These pamphlets represent the faith of the undersigned. When Inmac was started, I committed my work unto the Lord. This personal commitment has continued to grow over the years. His blessings have been bountiful to us at Inmac.*
>
> *Faith is a very personal issue with a very personal God. God wants that all should come unto Him. But He does not force the relationship, although He could if He wished. He asks that each one make his own decision about*

*Him, who His Son is, and what He did for us
on the cross some 2,000 years ago. He has done
a lot for me, and I give Him the glory for all
He has done.*

*How does this strong, personal position
benefit you as a vendor, employee, or visitor of
Inmac?*

1. *Every attempt will be made to treat you
   fairly.*
2. *In all ways we desire to be an ethical and
   aboveboard company.*
3. *Everyone will be treated with respect and
   consideration.*
4. *Personal faith is a privilege and a very private matter. Your privilege and privacy in
   this area are absolutely respected.*
5. *If for any reason you are not treated according to these principles, such treatment is not
   intentional and will be redressed.*

*If anyone has any questions about these pam-
phlets or our policies, please feel free to pick up
the house phone and call me at extension 5003.*

Kenneth A. Eldred
CEO

An outraged employee approached me one day to voice her
objection to the tracts. She'd been secretly taking them from
the lobby, she informed me. I invited her into my office to
discuss the matter, and it soon became apparent that her
actions were the result of deep personal pain in her life. She
needed help but had been unwilling to accept that which God
was offering. By the end of our conversation, she'd decided to
take the helping hand he was extending. She prayed to God,
indicating her decision to become a follower of Jesus.

Many believers in business would say the spiritual value of their work lies in the opportunities it provides for evangelism—or even the income it provides for Christian ministries. While these by-products of secular employment are indeed valuable, a paradigm that ascribes spiritual value to these alone ultimately falls short. It leaves our work in the marketplace void of inherent value, leads to a lack of fulfillment and joy in our everyday work, and contributes to the compartmentalized life. Those whose view of work life ministry encompasses only a ministry *at* work miss out on other important aspects of the ministry God gives those in the business world.

2. The Ministry of Work

We need to realize that God really does care about the work we do and how we do it: selling insurance to meet a need, caring for patients with compassion, building software solutions that enhance creativity, teaching children with excellence, or developing quality homes. He cares about our ministry *of* work. Our work *itself* is ministry to which we are called. It is holy and ordained by God.

Through our work we further God's own goals and serve his purpose through service and creation. Some of us spend our workdays making sure our company's financial records are accurate. Some of us design marketing campaigns. Some of us manage a team of executives. Some of us evaluate business ideas in order to assist the most promising ventures. Whatever we do, we're serving somebody, creating something, or most likely, doing both. That work itself is ministry, performed with excellence to the glory of God.

My friend Joey Burns sells real estate, mostly large land deals. I met him as he was on the other side of a transaction I was making. As a Christian, Joey is concerned not only to sell the property but to make sure the buyer was fully aware of the pluses *and minuses* of the property. He trusts God will bring the right buyer along, and he will not need to force the sale. When that negotiation was ended, I asked him to represent me on future land deals, because he put the interests of the clients on both sides ahead of his own. Joey is one of the few real estate people I know who has done many deals where he is the sole representative for the transaction—and at the conclusion of the deal both the buyer and the seller were very satisfied. He has a powerful ministry of work as he serves people with competence and integrity to the glory of God.

3. The Ministry to Work

Some of us are placed in positions of leadership, others of us aren't. No matter where we sit on the organizational chart, we've got an opportunity and responsibility to effect change, to act as redeeming agents in our spheres of influence. As we strive to improve organizational structures and policies, as we influence the way business is done, we are engaged in a ministry that's loaded with spiritual value. It's our ministry *to* work.

We have a significant role and responsibility in bringing God's ways to the organizations and industries in which we're placed—the businesses, markets, partners, schools, hospitals, governments, and churches in which we operate. It may involve working to remedy dishonest industry practices, unjust employment policies, or ignoble corporate cultures. Our ministry _to_ work involves being transformational agents in and of the marketplace. It involves impacting and transforming business *itself*.

John Sage met Chris Dearnley at Harvard Business School. A former Microsoft executive, John sought a way to support a ministry to at-risk children his good friend Chris ran in Costa Rica. The result was Pura Vida, a Seattle coffee company founded in 1999. It not only raises awareness and funding to the Costa Rican ministry, but also seeks to transform the way farmers in Costa Rica are treated. Pura Vida's commitment to 100 percent fair trade coffee ensures that farmers and producers receive living wages. By insisting on organic, shade-grown beans, Pura Vida ensures that the natural habitat they live in is preserved. John has a powerful ministry to work, as he strives to transform the prevailing practices of the Costa Rican coffee industry.

Redeeming Business

I've found there's widespread doubt in the church that the practice of business can be redeemed. Many take their cues from Augustine, who, leaning on pre-Christian Greek philosophy, stated that "business is in itself evil."[53] Their worldview is this: Business is business; it is inherently unspiritual and cannot be redeemed.

Of course, this idea is absurd if we stop to think about it. A farmer may buy a field that is unused. It is fallow and without water. He then goes to work to prepare the soil, provide irrigation, and plant crops. He redeems the land from its former lack of usefulness to a great garden for the good of all. On a visit to the Middle East a couple of years ago, I traveled across the Jordan River Valley. The Jordan River separates Israel from Jordan, and the two sides of the river offer a stark contrast. There are certainly many political issues in the region. However, the eastern side belonging to Jordan resembles a dust bowl. The Israeli side was likewise a desert when Israel became a state in 1947, but after much hard work, the land is now green. It's been redeemed. The contrast is actually breathtaking. You can literally see the national border based on the color change in the valley.

Business is like land. It is an asset. It can be worked for a purpose. That purpose could be noble or it could be ignoble.

Businesspeople are like farmers; they must take the asset and redeem it for the purpose of helping others and glorifying God. My friend Brett Johnson calls it "repurposing business," transforming a company into a vehicle for serving others to the glory of God. His organization *rēp* helps leaders "rethink every aspect of the operating model of an organization, examining things in light of eternal truths."[54] Brett's passion is redeeming businesses and people. In fact, the redeemed must redeem business.

You might be saying to yourself; "I can't possibly change the company or organization where I am working. After all, who am I?" That's just the point. You're God's representative. You are there for a purpose. If he has placed you there, he will help you succeed as you operate in faith to serve him in the work you are doing.

Called to Business With a Threefold Ministry

So we have a threefold ministry in our work life: pointing those around us to God (a ministry *at* work), serving and creating via the work itself (a ministry *of* work), and redeeming the practices, policies, and structures of institutions (a ministry *to* work). That's a pretty lofty charge for those of us in the marketplace!

Think about how these might play out in your work situation. Let's say you create advertising campaigns. In the course of your business, you will encounter those who are in need of encouragement, advice, and spiritual guidance. You have the opportunity to shed the wisdom of God's Word and share the redemption of Jesus with people around you (ministry *at* work). The advertising campaigns you produce, the way you deliver them, and the manner in which you meet the needs of your company or clients also reflect your faith. By bringing expertise, creativity, intelligence, and attitude to your work, you're serving your "customer" to the glory of

God (ministry *of* work). You also have the opportunity to take a stand against deceptive or misleading advertising—and certainly to refuse to engage in such practices yourself. As a believer, you can have a profound influence on how your trade is practiced and what ethical standards are embraced (ministry *to* work).

Sadly, much of business today lacks the fragrance of Jesus because we haven't picked up on our threefold ministry as priests in the marketplace. And part of the reason we haven't discerned our proper role is because we've lost sight of the church's primary role as a redeeming influence in the world. Many churches have focused on impressive and moving worship services on Sunday that have little carryover into Monday, leaving us ill equipped for our marketplace ministries. If the church is going to properly support our work life ministries, it needs to change the present model. It needs to be transformed from a cruise ship to an aircraft carrier.

CHAPTER 9

Unmasking the Common Goal of Church and Business

In nothing has the church so lost her hold on reality as in her failure to understand and respect the secular vocation.

(Dorothy Sayers, author, 1949)

Our work is not something that interferes with genuine spirituality; it is integral to what it means to be a Christian.

(Dr. Gordon T. Smith,
author and theologian, 2006)

If the gap between Sunday and Monday is going to be effectively bridged, the church scattered will need as much emphasis as we have given the church gathered.

(Dr. Ray Bystrom, professor of
pastoral ministries, 1995)

Neglecting Your Work

"How can anyone remain interested in a religion which seems to have no concern with nine-tenths of his life?" asks British author and Christian apologist Dorothy Sayers.[55] About 2,000 people who regularly attend church and who call themselves Christians were asked, "Have you ever in your life heard a sermon, read a book, listened to a tape, or been to a seminar that applied biblical principles to everyday work issues?" More than 90 percent of those surveyed said they never had.[56]

In its various forms, work is mentioned more than 800 times in the Bible. That's more than worship, music, praise, and singing combined.[57] Unfortunately, this significant and highly important aspect of our lives is receiving short shrift in the church. The silence leaves us with the impression that secular work is unspiritual and of no importance to God. Even worse, we're often left with the perception that business and faith are pulling in opposite directions.

What I didn't understand is that the real goal of business is aligned with the mission of the church. Business and church needn't stand opposed or compartmentalized; they can work together toward a common goal of serving others to God's glory and advancing his kingdom. In fact, the church has an extraordinary opportunity to affirm, equip, and commission working believers to important spheres it labors to reach. But I also didn't understand that doing so will require churches to rethink their assumptions and change the way they do their business. In this chapter, I'll describe the current situation in the church, explain how the goals of business and church align, present a new paradigm for the church, and provide examples of a few churches that are already deeply ministering to people's work life. So fasten your seat belts!

The Damage of the Greeks

Several years ago, a respected pastor blessed one of my grandsons, Nathaniel. "He will become a great pastor!" He made this pronouncement over the infant in a manner that evoked images of Simeon and the baby Jesus. We were over-joyed. A pastor! Then it struck me. It was so subtle, but I had succumbed to it. Why did I consider the prospects of my grandson's future as a pastor more special than a future as a businessman whose ministry was to serve others and share the gospel through business? After years of understanding that my calling was to the ministry of business, I had nev-ertheless succumbed to the all-too-prevalent work hierarchy that considers full-time employment in the church more spiritual than secular vocations.

The elevation of work in the "ministry industry" over work in other industries is so pervasive in the church that it's easy to revert to the sacred–secular hierarchy. But, as author and pastor A. W. Tozer notes in his classic book *The Pursuit of God*, the "sacred–secular antithesis has no foundation in the New Testament."[58] Instead, it's an idea borrowed from Greek philosophy. "In the fifth century A.D., Augustine sought to merge Platonic thought into a Christian framework," notes John D. Beckett in *Loving Monday*. "This approach resulted in a distinction between 'contemplative life' and 'active life' … between higher and lower." Taking his cues from Plato, Augustine placed secular work and occupations in the lower realm, inferior to the higher realm's sacred, church-related concerns.[59] And for the most part, the church has held to this aspect of Greek thought throughout history.

Unfortunately, this sacred–secular dualism we inherited from the Greeks has been one of the greatest barriers to the integrated life. It divides our spiritual life and work life in different categories on separate planes, and it also elevates church-related occupations above those in the marketplace. There's no avoiding the truth: The church's prevailing sa-cred–secular worldview and silence on work life matters has left those of us in the marketplace as damaged goods in at least four significant ways:

- First, the sacred–secular divide *leaves us conflicted and lacking joy and fulfillment in our daily work.* A. W. Tozer calls "the common habit of dividing our lives into two areas—the sacred and the secular— ... one of the greatest hindrances to the Christian's internal peace."[60] We feel caught in an irreconcilable position, trying to harmonize the demands of our jobs with those of our faith, resulting in a lack of internal peace, joy, and fulfillment.

- Second, the prevailing work hierarchy furthermore *robs us of a sense of calling to the business world.* Dallas Willard explains it as follows in *The Spirit of the Disciplines*: "There is truly no division between sacred and secular except what we have created. And that is why the division of the legitimate roles and functions of human life into the sacred and secular does incalculable damage to our individual lives and the cause of Christ. Holy people must stop going into 'church work' as their natural course of action and take up holy orders in farming, industry, law, education, banking, and journalism with the same zeal previously given to evangelism or to pastoral and missionary work."[61] We see ourselves as second-class Christians whose work lacks redemptive qualities and keeps us from serving God. We lack the realization that business can be our calling and our ministry.

- Third, when we believers compartmentalize our lives, or even abandon the business world altogether, we *fail to be redeeming agents in the marketplace.* We're familiar with the concept of redeeming people, but leaders of the local church rarely speak of redeeming business, our ministry *to* work. Yet that is an important function of believers in the marketplace. The church, says Dorothy Sayers, "has allowed work and religion to become separate departments, and is astonished to find that, as a result, the secular work of the world is turned to purely selfish and destructive ends, and that the greater part of the world's intelligent workers have become irreligious, or at least, uninterested in religion."[62] Left with the impression that our work inherently lacks spiritual value, we spend no time trying to figure out how to make that work effective for God. And thus we fail to become a redeeming influence in the business world.

- Finally, sacred–secular thinking also *relegates a large part of the church to the sidelines.* Many church leaders, perhaps unsure of the redemptive qualities of secular work, are kept from considering how to work with those in careers. As a result, the ministry of the church falls largely on those deemed called to, equipped for, and working in ministry.

Working Toward the Same Goal

Church and business are commonly perceived to be pulling in different directions—toward God and mammon, toward the sacred and the secular. I believe the disconnect we find today results in large part from a limited or misunderstood view of both the mission of the corporate church and the objective of business. Let me explain how they actually align.

The church has two dimensions that are interrelated yet distinct: *the outside mission of the church scattered* (daily public living and ministry in the world) and *the inside mission of the church gathered* (worship, teaching, and fellowship). "Unfortunately, there is a tendency in many Christian circles to emphasize one dimension of the church to the exclusion of the other," observes Ray Bystrom, professor of pastoral ministries. "Often, the focus is on the church gathered to the neglect to the church scattered." [63] The focus is on the church's inside mission (worship, teaching, fellowship) to the neglect of the outside mission.

Here on earth, the church has been tasked with a threefold mission relative to our fellow man. We are to (1) demonstrate the love of Christ by caring for people's needs (James 1:27), (2) proclaim the good news about Jesus (Mark 16:15), and (3) build disciples of Jesus in their faith (Matt. 28:19–20).[64] Some individual congregations or denominations place the emphasis on a subset of these, perhaps by focusing primarily on evangelism or by making social justice their mission. But Jesus really left us with a threefold task of loving, proclaiming, and discipling.

Simply stated, the threefold mission of the church gathered or scattered boils down to this: serving others (meeting different needs) to the glory of God. We serve others by meeting their physical, economic, and social needs. We serve others by sharing the good news of salvation through Jesus and thus being salt and light. We serve others by teaching them and leading them to spiritual growth. And the overriding principle is that whatever we do should be entirely for the glory of God (1 Cor. 10:31). Indeed, the first question of the Westminster Catechism asks, "What is the chief end of man?" The answer it provides: "Man's chief end is to glorify God, and to enjoy him forever." So to summarize, the mission of the church is *to serve others to the glory of God*.

Sound familiar? You'll recall that, properly understood, the goal of business is likewise to serve others to the glory of God. Can it be that the church and business really have congruent missions? I submit that they do. We can serve others to the glory of God whether he's placed us in a church, in a soup kitchen, in an office building, in a factory, or in a store. Regardless of the venue or role, our ministry is to love, proclaim, and disciple for God's glory. The church and business have the same objective and should be pulling in the same direction. But to make that a reality, I believe the church will ultimately need to change its paradigm.

Rediscovering the Role of the Church

Churches now have great multimedia presentations, talented musicians, gifted speakers, and top-notch audio systems. While the desire for a better in-church experience isn't wrong, there are usually undesired consequences:

- Regular attenders view "church" as the building rather than the people.
- The church building, not the world, is viewed as the center of the mission.
- The kingdom of God is portrayed as being centered at the gathered church for a few hours a week rather than when believers are deployed into the culture as salt and light.
- The model for evangelism is to bring seekers to church, where they'll be exposed to the gospel.
- The ministry of the church is seen as the role of relatively few, often paid by the church.
- The church worship service is an end in itself, not a means to an end.
- Many churchgoers see themselves as spectators rather than participants.
- There is a deep disconnect between Sunday's worship events and Monday's work realities.

When the early church moved their worship from the last day of the week to Sunday, the first day of the week, they made a profound theological statement—one that we need to recover today. The gathering of believers was not an isolated event but rather a launching pad for their ministries in the world. "For the church of that time had an outward-moving mission," notes Bystrom. "Sunday was not a day for escape; it was a day for preparation."[65] Dr. Howard Hendricks of Dallas Seminary agrees: "The New Testament church was primarily called to be a school, a training ground, a place for the equipment of saints to do the work of the ministry ... Today we reverse those arrows. Instead of going out, we have constituted the church as a soul-winning station."[66]

You may have heard the statement "the church is not a house of saints but a hospital for sinners." There's a valuable point in that, but it also leaves us with the impression that the place where people will find Jesus is inside the walls of the church. If the church is a hospital for sinners, the church building and gatherings are the key to getting people saved and healed. The pastor acts as a first-line triage agent and the church becomes a place of recovery.

We generally take our cues from pastors who often concentrate on an inside mission and assume that it's in the church where folks should be ministering. Indeed, when we're equipped for ministry, it's largely for activities within the church. Yet Jesus taught a very different model. He took his disciples with him to the cutting edge of culture (not "inside the church") where he applied the word of God. Then Jesus instructed and commissioned the disciples to do likewise. Sadly, many of us fail to engage our culture and pursue our mission in the world. Many pastors do, but I believe more of them need to start leading by example in this area. We need to recognize and take up the outside mission God has for us and the church.

Converting Cruise Ships to Aircraft Carriers

In order for the church and business to work together toward a common goal of serving others to God's glory and advancing his kingdom, the church must regain its focus on and function of equipping its ministers in the marketplace. Former business entrepreneur Doug Spada founded the non-profit venture WorkLife to support the church in this area. After a decade-long career serving on naval nuclear submarines and many successful years in business, Doug experienced the Sunday–Monday disconnect and found himself completely frustrated and unable to relate with his church. Out of that discontent was birthed a vehicle that would bridge the gap between the church and believers like him in the workplace. This was a new paradigm for the church to regain its purpose to primarily equip believers for kingdom impact at work, where they spend the majority of their waking hours and have the majority of their influence with others.

Doug describes this new paradigm in churches as "converting from cruise ships to aircraft carriers." Here's what he means. Many churches have become like cruise ships. Those who attend are passengers. They're brought to the ship to be entertained and fed, then they return to their everyday lives. Instead of cruise ships, churches can aspire to become like aircraft carriers. Those on board aren't there for the program, they're there to be taught, equipped, and refueled for a mission. The important work is done off the aircraft carrier, as those who are prepared do battle wherever they're sent.

WorkLife has developed a proven process by which churches are realizing a lasting change of focus through ministry to members' everyday work. Understanding that developing another "program" would not create enduring change, Doug and his team are providing strategy, resources, tools, and coaching that are helping churches navigate this process.

Here are a couple of examples of this shift in paradigm and focus:

Church of the Apostles, Atlanta, Georgia

Venture capitalist Charlie Paparelli realized that most adults who come to faith in Jesus do so the way he did—outside the walls and programs of a church. Years ago, he was outwardly very successful in his business life, yet inwardly his personal life was falling apart. Charlie describes himself as a "functional alcoholic who would never darken the doors of a church" at the time.

Charlie found God through his work relationships, and his passion now is to help others reach people who similarly are alone and without God at work. He's played a leading role in an Atlanta prayer breakfast that caters to non-believing business people who would otherwise never visit a church. Attendees are placed in weekly groups based on their stated level of interest in or commitment to Jesus. It's proven to be a highly effective ministry.

Charlie was challenged to start and lead a WorkLife ministry within his congregation, the Church of the Apostles. That initiative, which has a goal of "equipping the saints for the work of the ministry" has had a far-reaching impact on the mission of the church. "The church can no longer be a cruise ship where passengers are along for the ride, but must become an aircraft carrier from which people are being sent into battle," concludes Dr. James Saxon, the director of evangelism. He challenged the congregation to reclaim their work life for the glory of God, noting that it's essential to blessing the culture and reversing the church's isolation from the culture.[67]

Discovery Church, Orlando, Florida

Discovery Church has gone to a new level of effectiveness through the efforts of business leader Jim Butler. Since it was founded in 1993, Discovery Church has been recognized as "one of the ten healthiest churches in America" and "one of the fastest-growing churches in the United States during the 21st century." It's grown into a vibrant 4,000-member nondenominational body with ten different weekly worship services on two campuses. Senior Pastor David Loveless has been named "one of the top 20 Christian leaders in the United States to watch."[68]

"The church should be equipping people not just for church ministry but to be kingdom ambassadors in the world," the pastor says. "I want every person working in the marketplace to know that what they're doing is just as important as what I'm doing." Loveless is unusual in his affirmation for people's business life. He's "a pastor with that DNA," observes Jim Butler, who also serves as Discovery Church's Worklife Pastor.

A survey at Discovery Church revealed that, although business people felt affirmed in their work life, they didn't feel equipped for it. That was the motivation for Discovery @ Work, "an opportunity to intentionally equip, affirm, and deploy believers to integrate biblical wisdom at work, develop godly character, and effectively leverage our influence with non-believers in the workplace."

With guidance and support from WorkLife, the ministry was launched with a sermon series that articulated how work fits into God's plan and how the workplace can be a place of personal growth and influence. The weight of the pulpit raised awareness of everyday work as a ministry and a calling. For the last message, the pastor encouraged everyone to come to church dressed as they would at work—business suits, police uniforms, nursing scrubs—and he concluded by praying for them and releasing them to their calling.

Jim Butler, who shepherds Discovery @ Work, believes that every ministry of the church should support people in their calling to the workplace. Instead of asking people to serve in their ministries, says Jim, pastors should be saying to business people, "How can I serve you in your ministry?"

One of the biggest pieces of feedback the pastors received from business people is that they're not being asked to do one more thing; instead, they're being challenged to apply a different paradigm to what they're already doing—working.

Jim's own journey is one of learning to integrate faith and business and discover the ministry value of the workplace. After several pastoral positions, he took his first "secular" job in telecommunications sales while pioneering a church in San Diego. He and his wife began to rethink their calling and concluded it was to the marketplace. Jim was top salesman eight of the nine years he spent at the regional long-distance company. He then launched TeleCHOICE, a telecommunications business he still runs today.

Discovery Church is keenly aware of the specific issues facing business professionals and entrepreneurs, which comprise the largest segment of the church's workers. To meet that need, the church is starting the Entrepreneur's Roundtable, a forum where business professionals and owners receive "the fellowship and tools to stay strong and true to their faith as they grow to become successful and effective in this highly stressful atmosphere."

David Loveless sees his pastoral role as encompassing four important tasks: (1) giving the church a vision for work as one of the primary places where God does spiritual formation, (2) mobilizing people into work life groups, (3) reordaining everyone in the church to be pastors "out there" where they're called to operate, and (4) affirming the spiritual value of certain occupations and praying over the people in those fields. And what's his overall take on the effort to affirm and equip them in their calling to business? "Business people can't grin any further north than they already do," Pastor Loveless reports. "Many people have never imagined this kingdom value of their work life. Others have intuitively suspected it and are excited to hear it articulated from the pulpit."

He recalls, "When Jim and I had a vision for this kind of ministry, we weren't aware of any working models in other churches." He can now count four or five other sizable churches that are intentional about affirming the ministry value of business. Jim Butler believes more pastors are taking this approach, and the movement to integrate work and faith is growing, but it hasn't yet reached a tipping point. Business people need patience as the church makes the transition, he urges.[69]

North Point Ministries, Alpharetta, Georgia

I'm encouraged by folks like Durwood Snead, missions pastor in suburban Atlanta, who recognizes the important ministry and calling of business people in his church:

"We have 17,000 ministers at North Point Ministries. Most of them are business people. They are chosen by God, doing the work that God called them to do, and ministering around people outside the faith every day. As a paid church staff member, I need to look for opportunities to interact with outsiders. Our business people do it as a course of living every day. Many of them are hosting lunch meetings, showing DVDs of helpful messages, and then just discussing life with their co-workers. Their work is their ministry ...

"[Our] business ministers do not see a distinction between the sacred and the secular in their businesses. They see their businesses as ministries and their ministries as sacred. They look at the skills and experiences God has given them as perfect training and preparation for what God has for them to do next. And what an impact they are having.

"We are excited about the potential of thousands of our business people discovering what God has planned for them. You see, we believe God created business as one of his tools to usher in the kingdom. Our staff regularly reads business books to glean the truths in them experiencing what our business ministers are learning. But our role is simply to encourage, facilitate, and stimulate them as they bring the truth of the gospel to the workplace here and overseas."[70]

Individual followers of Christ in the marketplace may adopt the new paradigm, but there won't be a sea change in the church until more pastors like these internalize it, until they start asking followers of Jesus to share about their calling and ministry *in business*, until they validate *business people's work* as "full-time ministry," and until they commission business people *to the marketplace*. If that is to become part of their DNA, many churches must transform from cruise ships to aircraft carriers.

Business Leaders and the Current Paradigm

The sacred–secular paradigm has grown deep roots in today's church. Breaking those bonds constitutes a significant challenge. But as Nehemiah identified with the sin of the entire national of Israel, so business leaders must also identify with the problem of the existing cruise ship paradigm. To be sure, pastors and church staff have contributed to the current approach—but so have business leaders. We've been part of building and sustaining many of our cruise ship churches, not demanding a more biblical paradigm and metrics of success beyond attendance, budgets, and buildings.

Consider being part of the solution by sharing the integrated life vision and the potential to have your church effectively equipping believers for kingdom impact in the marketplace. WorkLife reports that approximately 80 percent of churches that transition to the aircraft carrier paradigm do so through the advocacy and vision of a business leader who leveraged his relational capital with church leadership. Our friends at WorkLife can draw on years of experience to assist your advocacy to your church leadership.

Practicing the Integrated Life

We started our journey by describing the workplace forces and internal tensions that lead us to compartmentalize our lives by segregating work, faith, and family. We then examined and corrected some misguided beliefs and attitudes that stem from our business education and church teaching and serve to compound the problem of separating our faith and work. God's plan is for us to live an integrated, abundant life.

It is to the integrated life in which work and faith are deeply connected that we now turn. It's time to put the new paradigm into practice. In the next Part, I will give you ways and examples of how it is done.

PART IV

Increasing Your Spiritual Joy While Impacting Your Work

Oswald Chambers said, "The spiritual manifests itself in a life which knows no division into sacred and secular." But what does an integrated business and spiritual life look like? How do we transform our compartmentalized lives into integrated ones? And how do we increase the spiritual impact of our lives at work?

In this Part, the rubber meets the road. We'll learn how to live a more integrated life and increase the impact of our threefold work life ministry. What can we do to increase our ministry *at* work? (Chapter 11) And how can we increase our ministry *of* work? (Chapter 12) But to kick it off, we'll reveal the key to supercharging the spiritual impact of our work lives. (Chapter 10)

CHAPTER **10**

Partnering with God to Leverage Your Results

God is looking for people through whom He can do the impossible—what a pity that we plan only the things we can do ourselves.

(A. W. Tozer, author and pastor)

Expect great things from God; attempt great things for God.

(William Carey, missionary)

If God is your partner, make your plans big.

(D. L. Moody, evangelist)

Believe and Trust

Imagine you're hurrying to leave for work one morning when your phone rings. You glance at the caller ID and notice it's an out-of-state number. After debating whether to risk being late for the third time this week, you finally decide to answer—with the intention of returning the call if it's really important. A voice on the other end says your name in a questioning manner. "Yes, what can I do for you?" you reply hurriedly. His answer changes the whole atmosphere of the morning. You decide to take a seat.

The caller is the legal representative of a relative you knew as a child but haven't seen in some time. You seem to recall he was a very successful businessman. This relative, you're told, just updated his will and left you his entire estate. The estate is sizable, but there are a number of instructions you must read, understand, and follow if you are to inherit it all. Now you're going to be very late for work, but suddenly that seems less important. After thirty minutes, you're more confident the caller is telling the truth. Some instructional material will be mailed to you, he explains. Promising to read it, you end the call.

A book arrives by overnight delivery the next day with a very warm, cordial, loving letter conveying both the affection of the long-lost relative for you and the undying support of the lawyer. The book is rather thick and appears daunting. But you open to the first page. "I encourage you to read the whole book for my sake and yours. Here's a quick executive summary: Believe that my estate exists for you. Believe that I will meet your needs. Trust me and love those around you. Trust that I will make up what you lack and provide for your good and for your current and future welfare. You are my heir, and as you seek my counsel and do what I ask, I will make sure that you are honored and cared for." Wow! Did you just hit a gold mine—or is it all too good to be true? But I bet you'll start studying the book carefully!

Of course, you've likely figured out that this story is alluding to all that God has for those who follow him. God's promises and gifts are enormous! "I tell you the truth, anyone who has faith in me will do what I have been doing," Jesus promised. "He will do even greater things than these, because I am going to the Father" (John 14:12). After Jesus returned to the Father, God placed the Holy Spirit within each of his followers. That's the power of God to work in us and through us. It's within our grasp, ours to take hold of.

"You can be a believer yet act as though there is no God," says Os Hillman, president of Marketplace Leaders. "Whenever you fret over life circumstances, you immediately demonstrate unbelief. Whenever you move out of fear or anxiety, you believe a lie about God's nature. Each day your actions affirm or convict you of your belief system. It reveals who the central focus of your life really is—you or God. It reveals who you place your ultimate trust in—you or God."[71] A friend who'd realized his ultimate trust needed to be in God rather than in himself once wrote, "I believe the solution to work and problems is not to work harder but to trust more." He's absolutely right.

We see incredible promises once we strip away the limits we put on God's Word. Our job is to believe it and live it—full speed ahead. Yet we do not always take him up on the promises and appropriate the power he has given us. The bottom line is this: If we are to live more integrated lives, we need to truly believe and trust God's promises.

Allow God to Be Your Partner

One of my earliest connections of Sunday to Monday was when I started "taking the Lord to work." Already praying for God to intervene in my work, I decided to invite Jesus to ride with me in the car on the way to the office. It struck me we were partners, and we lived at the same address—why not invite him along to carpool? I don't know about you, but when I ask someone into my car, I clear a place for my guest if there's stuff in the passenger seat. That's exactly what I did. As we drove down the road, I talked about what lay ahead during the day and sought his advice. Taking the Lord to work had a profound impact on how I perceived his interest in my business.

Of course, God doesn't need my car seat to get to my office. The act of inviting him to carpool was for me. It was a reminder that I was not in this business alone; God was there with me. You, too, have a partner in your work—a most willing and most able partner.

Trust That He Is a Willing Partner

We're often assured that God cares about our spiritual life, our family life, our health, and our personal relationships. We also know that God cares about how we conduct our business. But does he really care about business outcomes? Is it right to ask him for that contract, customer, promotion, or event?

While God does not measure business success by profit and growth the way our society does, it does not imply that he's uninterested in our business outcomes. God is in the business of doing miracles to make up for where we fall short. That is not confined to outcomes in personal areas like health, faith, and relationships. God wants to answer prayers for outcomes in the business sphere as well. He is in the business of doing the outrageous so that there is no doubt about who should receive the credit.

The critical next step is to truly believe he wants to be your partner in your work. If you can't believe he is interested in your business, then you will not see any outrageous works of his hand in your business life. Jesus performed countless miracles during his time on earth, yet the level of unbelief kept him from doing mighty works in his own hometown (Mark 6:5–6). Your greatest stumbling block may be unbelief. If you do not believe God desires to partner with you in business, then you will not experience any miracles in your work. Nor will you step out in faith to make the changes which result in experiencing the miraculous.

That's not to say a high level of faith will necessarily bring about enormous success. God can bless a business in many ways (e.g., financially, relationally, influentially) to his own glory. But he can also choose to close a business and turn the attention of the owner in a different direction, again for his glory. Either way, he wants us to include him and pray for the direction and outcomes in our business.

"Trust in the Lord with all your heart and lean not on your own understanding; in all your ways acknowledge him, and he will make your paths straight" (Prov. 3:5–6). We need to believe and trust that God wants to partner with us in every area of our lives, including our work.

Trust That He Is an Able Partner

Consider the implications of God wanting to partner with us in our business. What a transformational thought! Here's what our partner brings to the table:

- He promises to provide us wisdom and insight (James 1:5).
- He promises to give us firm footing (Prov. 10:9).
- He promises to meet our needs and bless us (James 1:25).
- He promises to give us joy and peace (John 16:24, 33).

We have the creator of the universe, the God of infinite knowledge and wisdom desiring to partner with us in our work and willing to sit next to us as we go to work. I don't know about you, but that's an offer I can't imagine turning down!

As I was in the middle of writing a previous book, *God Is at Work*, I had lunch with a friend, a home remodeling contractor, who lamented the poor state of his business. I asked him if he had turned to God with his problem.

"I didn't want to bother the Big Guy," he replied. "I only ask him for personal strength and courage to do what is right."

"You've got the wrong idea about God," I told him. "God *wants* to be involved. He wants to be a testimony in your life. He wants to partner with you."

The light seemed to go on. "I get it," he said, "I'm only getting half of the equation. The other half in my business is God."

"Yes, but it's even more dramatic than that," I replied. "Your approach is like running a car or truck on one cylinder when there are seven more available. And then we wonder why it's not working well!" He understood the message and began to pray about his business.

I caught up with him a couple of years later. "Have you been praying, and what has God been doing in your business," I asked. Beaming, he told me how God had blessed with an abundance of new business. Things turned around so much that he had to be selective about which projects to take. He tells everyone who will listen about God's goodness and answers to prayer. He went from being a nominal believer to a walking testimony to God's love and faithfulness for him.

Let God Direct Your Path

We have a very eager and very capable partner. I came to the realization early on that he wasn't just my partner but my senior partner. So when we started and incorporated Inmac, I did not fill the seat of Chairman of the Board. I made the Lord Chairman. Inmac's public offering document listed our board members, but none as Chairman. That seat was left to God. It was an act of surrendering the business to my senior partner.

God doesn't want to be a junior partner we consult on occasion—he wants to be the controlling partner. When you let him direct your path, things will start to happen. Begin the day spiritually prepared, read his word, pray specifically, and leave room for him to work. You'll be amazed at how your willing and able senior partner meets your needs at work.

Start Every Day With a Clean Slate

Perhaps the greatest lesson I learned in business is the power of starting each workday spiritually prepared. About two years after we decided to follow Jesus, my company Inmac was just getting off the ground. One of our board members owned a small direct-mail business in a different field. We'd relied heavily on that company's expertise for guidance, as the same skills were required in his business as in ours.

All that changed when he saw our success and decided to sell computer-related products. He had taken what he'd learned at Inmac to now establish a directly competing business! Furthermore, his position as a board member gave him insight into our business plans, while we at Inmac were blinded to his company's strategy.

Given his actions, I now clearly saw him as an adversary with an unfair advantage. I knew I had to do something. I had no way of removing him from our organization, as our legal documents never anticipated such a situation. This board member was a very powerful individual and could make life really difficult. I was upset. Our relationship was becoming more and more strained, so I set up an appointment with him.

During the days before the meeting, my wife Roberta and I sought guidance through prayer. In the process, Roberta found a Scripture that related directly: "When a man's ways are pleasing to the Lord, he makes even his enemies live at peace with him" (Prov. 16:7). We claimed this verse as we prepared a solution to our problem: I would ask the board member to leave Inmac's board immediately, sell his shares back to our existing shareholders at a reasonable price, and accept a promissory note with minimal interest, to be paid off in one year without any real collateral. My offer certainly wasn't going to make him leap for joy, but it was the best we could come up with. There really weren't many options available to us. This man could decide to say no—after all, he was in a strong position. What a predicament!

With trepidation, I walked into his office at the appointed time. We exchanged some pleasantries before I came to the point of the meeting. I laid out our proposal, looked down, and waited for what might be the worst. It was silent for what seemed like forever, but when I looked up he was smiling at me. I must have looked surprised, because he smiled all the more! I almost fell off my chair when he said, "I think that's a reasonable solution to our dilemma. Let's draw up some papers and get this done." Needless to say I was overjoyed and immediately thought back to that verse we'd been claiming. We thanked God for going before me and preparing the way. The adversarial relation ended, and we remained friends even though our companies ended up competing.

So I determined to commit the issues of the day to God before leaving for work. Roberta and I would have coffee together and talk about the day ahead. We would look at my schedule, and then we would look at hers. We'd consider who would be at meetings, what the issues were, and what problems we might expect. We would even talk about specific people we might encounter during the day. Then we'd commit all of that to prayer.

Scripture tells us to ask if we lack wisdom, and God will give it to us abundantly (James 1:5). When we ask in the morning, God promises to answer. Prepare yourself spiritually for each workday, and at the end of your prayer time, get up and walk, knowing God will participate with you and give you what you need when you need it. Spiritual preparation includes five important components:

1. *Confessing our shortcomings.* The cleansing of sin is the precursor to being used by God in mighty ways (Isa. 6:5–8).

2. *Putting on the whole armor of God:* truth, righteousness, peace, faith, salvation, Scripture, Holy Spirit. It's essential if we hope to stand our ground against Satan's schemes (Eph. 6:10–18).
3. *Asking God to be our partner.* We must remember his place and submit to him.
4. *Coming before God to seek his counsel and direction.* We have the God of the universe available to show us the way.
5. *Being filled with the Holy Spirit every day (Eph. 5:18), sensing his presence, so he may lead us.* Moses said to God, "If your Presence does not go with us, do not send us up from here" (Ex. 33:15). God must go before us.

First Study the Manual

If we're going to let God direct our path, we need to know his promises and commands intimately—and this means we must read his Word. Take the time to study the manual, especially as it relates to your work. Approach God's Word without any preconceived notions, allowing the Holy Spirit room to operate. I try to spend 30 to 60 minutes each morning reading Scripture, and I've found that my daily study often directly applies to situations and decisions throughout the workday. Because they watched me as they were growing up, my sons picked up this habit of daily study too. Whether the issues are minor or have significant implications, it's important to know God's Word on the matter and trust his instruction.

Pray Specifically

Many people, like my friend the remodeling contractor, offer very vague prayers. When our prayers are indefinite, it's impossible to see clearly the hand of God. I have found that we must learn to pray very specifically for what we think we need or the specific problem we need solved. Then we'll see him answer in unmistakable ways. Here's one example from my business career.

After we started the company, Inmac's sales took off like a rocket—from $0 to $50,000 total in three months. Then after six months, the company suddenly started to struggle. We'd invested everything we owned in the business. We had even given personal loan guarantees. I was worried. Maybe this wasn't God's plan for me? Perhaps he wanted me to pursue another venture? Or did he want me to become a pastor after all? When things go south, these types of questions frequently enter our minds.

My wife Roberta and I decided to put the question of my continued involvement with Inmac before God. I sought an answer that was unmistakably from him. In the Bible, Gideon put a fleece of wool on the ground at night, seeking an answer from God. Would he be with Israel in the upcoming battle? Gideon asked as a sign that the fleece would be wet while the ground remained dry. The next morning, he wrung out a bowl full of water from the fleece; the ground around was dry. Just to be sure it wasn't some episode of happenstance, Gideon then asked for the reverse—a dry fleece and wet ground. That night, God answered again, and Gideon was confident that Israel would win the battle (Judg. 6:36–40).

What would our fleece be? Inmac's daily sales had topped at $2,500, but they'd fallen about 20 percent from there—and it didn't look like we'd hit the bottom yet. So with sales at $2,000 per day and steadily drifting downward, Roberta suggested we pray that God would give us a $7,000 sales day as a sign. (We'd learned that seven was a number that signified perfection in the Bible.) "And not just one," she continued, "we'll ask for three $7,000 days!" I thought she was trying to outdo Gideon! Not wanting to seem unspiritual, especially in front of my wife, I agreed with the idea. But on the inside I was seriously concerned. How could God do something that incredible?

We committed to praying about it for ten days. I was terrified the first five days. Sales continued to drop. Then each day brought a greater belief that God had our best interest in store, whatever the outcome. Finally, we were both convinced God would touch our fleece and give us a $7,000 day.

The next morning, a Monday, I went to work and called a company meeting. All four employees turned up. I announced we would have a $7,000 day. Nancy, our customer service representative, looked at me with understandable doubt. With sales on a downward trajectory, she couldn't help but wonder if the boss had gone crazy. Perhaps the pressure was too much for him—he looked too excited in view of our sales situation. The others in the office had that distant look of "where did I put my résumé?"

Orders started coming in, and the day was looking pretty good. At about 2 p.m., Nancy walked into my office. "Things are going so well we might even reach $5,000 in sales," she announced gleefully. It was obvious she was trying to let me off the hook. I shook my head and reiterated, "No, Nancy, we're going to have a $7,000 day." After 2 p.m., orders continued steadily, and at 5 o'clock we got our last order—from Hawaii of all places, where it was two hours earlier in the day. Now we were all excited. Nancy ran a tally on our ten-key adding machine, as we could not afford a computer. When she'd double-checked the final end-of-the-day tally, it read just over $7,000! We were all blown away.

Those numbers were repeated the following two Mondays. Then sales returned back to their previous level of about $2,000 per day. But that was no longer worrisome. God had touched our fleece. He wanted me in that business, and he cared about it. He had affirmed my calling to Inmac—and to business in general! God had answered our specific prayer in an unmistakable way.

When we pray specifically, we know for certain God has answered our prayers. I would suggest you pray specifically, and keep a detailed record of your prayers. We often pray hastily and then go on our way. We can easily forget what we prayed for and later fail to recognize our partner's hand in all that is going on when he does answer. A prayer log helps us see patterns in our prayer life and patterns in his response. Our faith will be strengthened as we recognize and know for ourselves God's involvement in all aspects of our life. We will trust him more to direct our path.

Hold On to Your Work Loosely

We need to be focused on hearing God's voice, and we need to be open to turns in the road. That requires us to hold on to our work loosely. Many of us find that difficult in an environment where people are so vested in their jobs and so identified with their titles.

We must not get stuck on what we think our job should be and how long we should be there. The apostle James writes, "Now listen, you who say, 'Today or tomorrow we will go to this or that city, spend a year there, carry on business and make money.' Why, you do not even know what will happen tomorrow ... Instead, you ought to say, 'If it is the Lord's will, we will live and do this or that'" (James 4:13–15). James isn't telling us to simply tack the words "Lord willing ..." to the beginning of business plans we've devised solely on the basis of our personal capabilities and experiences. Instead, he's instructing us to invite our all-knowing partner to be part of our decision-making and planning. We need to hold on to our work loosely and be prepared for a change should that be God's plan.

When God started blessing our Inmac venture, I had big dreams. Most of them came to pass. As the company matured, I envisioned it becoming like a Hewlett-Packard, where my father had spent his career. I pictured a long legacy. But even as the company was growing and obviously experiencing God's blessing, I told him I realized there might come a day when his plans for me would change. "Just as you'd clearly shown me with the $7,000 days that you wanted me at Inmac, make it clear to me when you're ready to end my time at the company," I prayed. "When you do, I promise I will step down and not look back."

Even though I did not want that day to come, it eventually did. God made it obvious to me one day through my board members that it was time to step down. (I think the board was a bit surprised by my willing reaction.) When we hired a new president and CEO, I promised him I'd operate like a pair of training wheels on a bicycle. I would advise him only and slowly raise the wheels, giving him more and more latitude as he felt comfort and demonstrated skill to run the company.

Within six months, that role was over. I began to work on future projects while staying out of his way. A number of new employees were surprised at my willingness to back away. They remarked how unusual it was for an entrepreneur to let go of "his baby." For me, it was a matter of trusting God. I knew my status and well-being didn't depend on the company or my position in it but on who God was in my life. He'd brought me this far; he wouldn't let me down now. Don't hold too tightly to what you think you should be doing. Leave room for your partner to direct your path.

Trust Your Senior Partner for the Outrageous

God is willing and able to do the outrageous as our partner in business, but we've got to be willing and able to surrender to him, to allow him room to operate, and to trust that he can do it. Consider the story of Peter who saw God touch his business in a supernatural, outrageous way (Luke 5:1–11). A

trained and experienced fisherman, Peter had been unsuc-
cessful in catching fish all night, when Jesus commanded
him to put down his nets one more time. The tired Peter
complained, having just dried, repaired, and put away his
nets. It would just be a wasted exercise. After all, many years
of experience told him fishing in midmorning wouldn't work.
There's no specific light to attract the fish, the noise from the
shore drives them away, and they swim too deep when the
water's warmer. Plus, the fishing had already proven terrible
the entire night before—under better conditions.

Nonetheless, Peter chose to partner with Jesus and cast
his nets in the water again. And the results were quite different! So many fish filled the nets that they started to break. A
second boat had to be summoned to help carry the catch, and
even then both boats were loaded to such an extent that they
began to sink. Peter probably had more fish in one catch than
a week of fishing on his own would have yielded!

Peter was a good fisherman who knew the rules of fishing. The business had earned him a good living. But when
he trusted Jesus to lead, the result of the partnership was
explosive—it was outrageous. He knew God had shown up
at his office. The encouragement to his nascent faith was
phenomenal, and the testimony to those around him was
astounding.

Perhaps my most memorable experience of God's hand
unmistakably at work occurred Friday, October 10, 1986, the
day Inmac was scheduled to have its public offering. An IPO
is the holy grail of many an entrepreneur; it's seen as the
reward for years of hard work building a company. In our
case, it was the culmination of more than a decade of growing
Inmac and months of preparation to go public. We expected
the offering to go out with the opening of the New York Stock
Exchange (NYSE) at 9 a.m. Eastern Standard Time.

Shortly before the opening bell, our lawyer called to inform me that the Securities and Exchange Commission (SEC)

needed an explanation on one point relating to our public offering. The sale of stock to the public would net Inmac $10 million in cash, but the SEC couldn't determine why we'd need these funds given our very healthy balance sheet. They asked for a one-page letter describing our plans for the funds. By the time we faxed the response to the SEC's fax center on our lawyers' letterhead, it was 11:45 a.m. on the East Coast.

In the fall of 1986, the United States federal government was experiencing budget issues, and it decided to shut down at noon that particular Friday in an effort to save money. That included the SEC. The fax arrived fifteen minutes before closing time. "I cannot approve this offering today because the office closes at noon," replied the responsible SEC lawyer when reached by phone. "There simply isn't enough time to run down, get the fax, and issue a formal response." His conclusion was firm.

We were stunned. The prospect of the stock not going public that day was dreadful. Our investment bankers thought the soft, "choppy" market conditions wouldn't permit the stock sale for at least six weeks. Then we'd have to reapply for the public offering, essentially starting over. It would cost time, money, and effort, and investors would potentially view the company less favorably.

Something had to change, but the phone call with the SEC pointed to an inevitable, devastating outcome. This was a problem only God could solve. We had to lean on our partner, trusting that he was willing and able. With ten minutes left in Washington's workday, my wife Roberta and I laid out the problem before God like Hezekiah did. In a small, empty conference room at Solomon Brothers, we began to pray for a miracle, something outrageous that only God could deliver. Though it seemed impossible, we prayed that he would get our company on the public market that day. I didn't even want to speculate how he could possibly do that. From a natural perspective it seemed hopeless.

As we were praying, we heard a startling announcement over the loudspeaker on the trading floor at Solomon Brothers: The U.S. government's official closing time had been pushed back to 1 p.m. Wow! The same God who stopped the sun for a day in response to Joshua's prayers (Josh. 10:12-14) kept the federal government open an extra hour as we prayed.

We placed another call to the SEC lawyer, who now had the time to issue a favorable response. Inmac's IPO was approved by the SEC at 12:03 p.m. We'd leaned on our willing and able partner, and he came through big-time! All the glory went to our outrageous God.

We have a tremendous resource available to us in our daily work: our almighty God is willing and able to help us! Our work can be highly leveraged by partnering with him. He can supercharge our spiritual impact! But we need to submit and let him direct our path. We need to make him the controlling partner.

As mentioned earlier, we have a threefold work life ministry—ministry *at*, *of*, and *to* work. In the next three chapters, we'll explore specific ways we can improve the spiritual impact of these three. How can we better glorify God in relation to ourselves, our co-workers, our customers, our employers, and our industry? I'll explain how.

CHAPTER 11

Living Your Faith at Work

The fruit of the Spirit is love, joy, peace, patience, kindness, goodness, faithfulness, gentleness and self-control.
(Galatians 5:22–23)

A word aptly spoken is like apples of gold in settings of silver.
(Proverbs 25:11)

[I] did not come to be served, but to serve.
(Jesus Christ, Matthew 20:28)

Invest in Your Work for God's Glory

Many are too uninvolved in their work, perhaps because they view their work activity as a means to do something else. It provides the resources to do what they really want to do. I'm sure you've heard people say, "I hate my job, but how else am I going to pay the bills?" This attitude leads the person to withdraw from work and "just do time," thereby cheating himself and his employer. It is unbiblical and wrong.

If our work is our calling, we should find joy and meaning in it. If our work is our ministry, it should be personal and excellent. If we're going to point others to God, we need to earn the right to be heard. We need to invest in our work for God's glory.

Find Joy and Meaning in Your Work

Our work needs to be meaningful to us personally. Nothing is more discouraging and uninspiring than a job we consider meaningless. A vile Nazi experiment in World War II showed this clearly. Two groups of prisoners were treated exactly the same except for their daily work assignments. One group was given meaningful work while a second was given futile work that involved moving mounds of dirt from one random location to another. As the mounds were transported daily between arbitrary locations selected by their captors, workers in the second group quickly despaired of their job as being meaningless. This gruesome study revealed that these individuals died more quickly than the others who had meaningful work. It's important that we find the value and meaning in our work.

It's also important to make the most out of our business day. Since our jobs comprise the prime waking hours of the day, we ought to spend that time on something we enjoy or can get passionate about. We should be able to do our work with a sense of personal involvement and accomplishment. God has prepared us to do what he calls us to do (Eph. 2:10), and we should be able to find joy in our work. Joy should be a part of our day. When we are happy with our work, we'll get involved in what we do. We'll excel in our work and make a serious contribution.

If you are unable to find happiness with what you do, or if you cannot find meaning in your work, you're not displaying the attitude Scripture mandates. If your attitude is bad and you find yourself constantly complaining even after taking it to the Lord, there is something fundamentally wrong, and you need to consider changing your employment. If you cannot find joy in your work, you're probably in the wrong place. You can and should change jobs. Yes, finding more fulfilling employment can be hard work, but it's much worse to stay where you are, doing what you do not like to do. Find work in which you enjoy using your gifts.

Earn the Right to Be Heard

Years ago, I had an employee who was very devout in her faith, a really sweet person. More than anything, she wanted to tell those around her about Jesus. She would go to the office kitchen during a break, catch colleagues in conversation, and interject her faith. She would stop people in the hall and share Jesus. She was not particularly discreet, and soon people began to avoid her in the halls and in the company kitchen.

Comments started coming back to me from other employees who found her annoying. They wondered if she had enough work to do. It turned out she wasn't getting her work done in the office, and the person she was working for, someone who didn't share her faith, was particularly disappointed in her performance. She was never one to stay late; her husband picked her up exactly as the workday ended. So if she was going to get her share of witnessing done, it would have to be during working hours!

Co-workers sought to avoid her because they had a lot of work to do, and she was keeping them from it. She never bothered to ask if it was the right time to talk. Soon she found herself somewhat isolated. Oblivious to her off-putting approach and attitude, she felt ostracized because of her faith.

The topic of witnessing in business elicits a shudder in most of us. Perhaps you've seen a misguided approach similar to the account above. If the truth be known, and we hate to admit it, we'd rather steer clear of sharing our faith in the workplace. It's awkward and difficult, and it seems so out of place and character with the business environment. We have visions of unwelcome Jehovah's Witnesses knocking on the door at the most inconvenient time with information nobody wants to hear.

How then should we convey our faith in a secular, business-hardened, postmodern cultural environment in which sharing Jesus seems awkward and out of place? In short, we need to earn the right to be heard, and we need to be mindful of the right time and place. Earning the right is hard work. It means doing your work with excellence and integrity, not stealing work hours from your employer to engage in witnessing. It means building relationships and getting in other people's shoes. It means helping co-workers or customers, perhaps even spending the extra hours to do so when your own work already requires the full day, because that time is part of your ministry, your calling.

Before Jesus preached, he performed many miracles. He met people's physical needs and in serving them created such a positive stir that people could not help but ask him questions. When he spoke about their spiritual needs, they were receptive to respond to the love of God. As followers of Jesus, we must get involved in our work for the sake of the gospel. By investing in our work, we will, as Paul says, "make the teaching about God our Savior attractive" (Titus 2:10). We need to earn the right to be heard—and then we should be bold yet judicious when God puts opportunities before us.

Put Aside Jealousy, Discord, Selfish Ambition, and Envy

One day you cannot help but overhear a colleague in conversation with the boss you share. "Joe, we've been watching you, and we're impressed with your work," the boss tells him. "We've decided to give you a promotion and raise your salary by 20 percent." *I can't believe it*, you think to yourself, *I've been here longer than Joe, and I do at least as much as he does! I've just been passed over; it's just not fair!* Or perhaps you run into an old classmate you haven't seen in years. As a student, this friend would sometimes come to you for academic help. But now, seeing him or her for the first time in years, it's apparent that you're in very different places. You've done okay, but your classmate has hit it big. The great vacations, the expensive car, the beautiful home ... you can't help but make an unfavorable comparison to your own situation. Your next thought is, *Why not me? That person is no better than I am.*

Jealousy, discord, selfish ambition, and envy are attitudes common in our society, and they're perhaps disproportionately found in the workplace. The Bible includes these attitudes in a laundry list of ingredients of the sinful nature with the warning that "those who live like this will not inherit the kingdom of God" (Gal. 5:19–21). They're ugly attitudes that keep us from the fellowship of Jesus and the partnership of the Holy Spirit.

Unfortunately, those who live with the mantra that business and religion don't mix sometimes rationalize unbiblical attitudes in their work lives, considering themselves excused from following the standard God gives for the rest of their lives. When our lives are compartmentalized, we more easily allow our work attitudes to be shaped by the prevailing culture, and in the business world that often includes jealousy, discord, selfish ambition, and envy. But we are not compartmentalized creatures, so we need to realize biblical mandates apply to all areas of our lives, including our work sphere.

The Bible calls the harboring of bitter envy and selfish ambition in our hearts wisdom that is "earthly, unspiritual, of the devil. For where you have envy and selfish ambition, there you find disorder and every evil practice" (James 3:14–16). These attitudes place the focus on ourselves rather than on a spirit of thankfulness to God. We consider ourselves the served rather than the servants. When we allow our selfish nature to rule instances at work, we lose our opportunity to be effective for God. What kind of a witness is a life at work marked by jealousy, discord, and so on?

I highlighted jealousy, discord, selfish ambition, and envy from the list of transgressions that mark the sinful nature because these have the greatest impact on our business outlook. In a competitive environment like the business world, we can easily stray from biblical norms into sinful attitudes. (Competition is fine, but as with most actions, attitude is everything.) When we approach others with a cutthroat, factious, callous, or jealous heart, we let sin rule our competitive nature. However, when we have a heart to better serve people in a spirit of love, mercy, peace, and humility, we're displaying biblical principles in the marketplace.

Be Salt and Light, Not Acid and Judgment

All of us who have operated in the workplace know it can be messy and filled with attitudes that fly in the face of biblical wisdom. How should we react when faced with stuff we know is unpleasing to God? In his famous Sermon on the Mount, Jesus said we are the salt of the earth and the light of the world. Our lives should exhibit saltiness and display light so that others "may see your good deeds and praise your Father in heaven" (Matt. 5:13–16). I've found salt and light to be the secret ingredients in the workplace as well.

In a recent sermon, a pastor friend told the following story relating to the workplace: A follower of Jesus ate lunch in his company's cafeteria. The guys around him knew he was a Christian and liked to goad him about his faith. He began his lunch as usual with a silent word of thanksgiving. Others walked up and sat at his table. One of them pulled out a copy of *Playboy* magazine, opened the centerfold, and passed it around to his friends. After a few minutes, one of them took the centerfold and shoved it in front of this dear brother. He looked at the picture as they had directed him to and continued on with his lunch. "Tell us, Mr. Goody-Goody, what did you see?" prodded one of the guys. He looked at them with a somber expression. "I see the face of a young lady who cannot be much older than her early twenties. I see a lost young lady who has fallen into an evil trap, a life that will lead her into pain and loss. I see a young lady whose father and mother are most likely deeply saddened by the exposure of their daughter in front of cameramen, directors, and others, and who is now publicly exposed for the world to see. I see a young lady who could be your daughter and wonder how you would feel if you saw her in this centerfold. I see a young lady who will have to explain this photo someday to the ones she loves. I see a very sad situation indeed." The men at the table quietly put the magazine away and never brought it out again. The truth spoken with compelling compassion is the salt and light I'm talking about.

Note that being salt and light and taking a stand are not the same as judging another person. "What business is it of mine to judge those outside the church?" Paul asks, going on: "God will judge those outside" (1 Cor. 5:12–13). The believer faced with hostile colleagues at lunch took a stand, but he didn't impugn the men around him or judge them. He brought light into the marketplace by being the preservative of salt. Sadly, many of us—and at times all of us—tend to be critical of others, believing that it's our job to help others see how they measure up in the light of God's Word. We are not called to deal harshly with those who don't agree with us. Instead, we must be patient, peaceful, and kind.

Being salt and light requires us to start our day in prayer and continue in prayer for guidance as we get hit by new situations. Any guidance we perceive from the Holy Spirit must agree with some simple biblical principles:

- Are you exhibiting the love of God with what you are about to say?
- Does what you are about to say shed the light of God according to the Scriptures on the subject?
- Will what you commit to or say cause you or someone else to be compromised relative to your or their Christian beliefs?

Treat All People with Dignity

Every person is unique. God has gifted them with abilities and has made them in his image. We are to recognize that fact, respect the creation he has made, and treat people with the dignity they deserve, whether they're walking with God or not. We must do our best to find the best in the people around us and give them praise for the things they do well. It doesn't mean that we whitewash issues, but we need to view and present those issues in the light of the rest of the individual's work and skills.

We need to take the time to learn about the people we work with and recognize that no job is too small. On a final exam at a major Christian university, the professor's last test question was the following: What is the name of the custodian who takes care of this building and keeps it so that we can use a well-kept facility? The students complained that the question had nothing to do with the material they'd covered in class. The professor responded that it may not be relevant to the course material, but without the custodian's constant care, the class would not have been the same. He was an integral part of the course.

We need to know those around us and serving us. Often, we don't take the time to get to know them and their needs. Not knowing their needs, we're unable to be the kind of support people often really need. Ivica Horvat, the son of a Baptist pastor, founded a business that manufactures work clothing and uniforms in his native Croatia. He is a beacon of integrity in a business climate pervaded by corruption. Within his company, Ivica is a shining example of Christ's love to employees. So deep is his interest and caring is his attitude toward others, that a non-Christian single mother in his employ stated, "Ivica is my pastor."

If we're going to have a ministry at work, we must get to know the people around us. If we're going to love, encourage, and offer God's truths, we need to know more than what they do on the job.

Give People the Grace to Make Mistakes

In the high-pressure world of business, it's hard to give people the latitude to make mistakes in their work. If a superior committed the error, we're often quick to criticize the boss, particularly in front of fellow employees. If it was a subordinate, we may take the error as an opportunity to dump our bucket of pent-up frustration or view their mistake as more debilitating than it really is.

Of course this does not mean that we ignore all errors. If a person commits the same error over and over again, then it's not a mistake—it's negligence. And if a person perpetrates an illegal or malevolent act without repentance, we must deal with it as it is and take the appropriate action.

When someone in my organization makes an honest mistake, I try to approach it with grace. The Lord has forgiven us for the sin in our lives and the mistakes we have made. Hopefully, I extend the same grace God has extended to me.

The Bible says we will be judged as we judge others. I go over the mistake to understand how it happened and what that employee learned from the error. The objective is a mutual understanding of why it will not happen again.

Silicon Valley looks at entrepreneurs differently than most other people around the country. If an entrepreneur's startup attempt has failed, the question is why. If the answer makes sense, the Valley sees that person as better, not worse, for having had the experience. As some wag once said, good judgment comes from experience, and experience comes from bad judgment.

Be an Encourager and Optimist

Attitude is everything. Too often we come to work with the weight of the world on our shoulders. It does not belong there. "Come to me, all you who are weary and burdened, and I will give you rest," says Jesus (Matt. 11:28). As followers of Jesus, we are to cast all our cares on him (1 Pet. 5:7). When we do, we are free to focus on others and be the encourager they need in their own work.

Sometimes it's issues at work that frustrate us. It's way too easy to fall prey to the typical gripe sessions that can take place in any office. Rather than falling into this pattern, encourage people to view the issues from another viewpoint. As an encourager, you're able to change the atmosphere in the group and begin the process of looking around for ways to solve whatever problem seems to be bringing on discouragement.

I wish I could say I am always good at being an encourager, but I'm not. When I find myself having a tough time putting on a positive outlook, I have a couple of Christian friends I like to turn to, including my wife Roberta, who can help me see the positive side. I've also found that exercise and sleep will help me get an issue back in perspective when I only see the negative. In the final analysis, we need to remember that God has a plan for our good and our welfare (Jer. 29:11). We need to trust he will carry it out.

No one ever fixed a problem by starting with the words *I can't.* An encourager is someone who has hope. The gospel is hope personified. "With God all things are possible," Jesus promised (Matt. 19:26). Hope is infectious and gets people thinking in a positive way to bring out the best in any situation—or in people who are dealing with seemingly hopeless situations. Hope is able to help us put everything in perspective. The CEO that I hired at Inmac dealt with every incredibly difficult situation by putting it in perspective. When something went wrong, he'd comment out loud, "Well, nobody died here." Then he would set out to find an answer.

There are many ways to apply the gospel to what we say and do at work. Indeed, it could well be a whole book. I have highlighted only a few points here. The objective is to be a witness of God's love by word and a reflection of God's love by deed. Many of those around us have little hope and tend to be up and down with the waves of life. As we stand strong in the promises of God, we will stand out like a strong tower. We will have earned the right to be heard, and people will wonder what enables us to stand in the difficult world of work.

Our work life ministry isn't just confined to **how we act** and **what we say at work** (our ministry *at* work). The **work we do, how we do it,** and **how well we do it** can have a powerful spiritual impact as well. Scripture exhorts us to be about "doing the will of God from your heart. Serve wholeheartedly, as if you were serving the Lord, not men" (Eph. 6:6–7). Let me explain how we can increase the spiritual value of our ministry *of* work—in other words, how we can increase the spiritual impact of the work we do and how we do it.

Chapter 12

Serving Others to the Glory of God

Each one should use whatever gift he has received to serve others, faithfully administering God's grace in its various forms.

(1 Peter 4:10)

Good is the enemy of great.

(Jim Collins, author & business consultant)

No task will be so sordid and base, provided you obey your calling in it, that it will not shine and be reckoned very precious in God's sight.

(John Calvin)

The Work You Do: Know Your Calling

In order to serve others most effectively, we need to know our calling. Simply put, if we're pursuing the wrong calling, we're not having the greatest spiritual impact through our work. To stay true to our calling requires us first to learn and understand our gifts and then to create and follow a mission statement aligned with those abilities.

Learn and Understand Your Gifts

God has hard-wired us with a set of talents and abilities. Some of us are great at sports; some of us are natural musicians; some of us are really good at teaching; and others are skilled in some aspect of business. I've seen these natural giftings described as different "intelligences": bodily-kinesthetic, interpersonal, linguistic, logical-mathematical, naturalistic, intrapersonal, spatial, musical.[72] Each of us has a set of intelligences. And when we commit our lives to Christ, we get an additional set of spiritual gifts that may relate to what we do.

Scripture makes clear we're not gifted in all areas (1 Cor. 12:28–30). Everyone's assignments, skills, and gifts differ to some degree. Along with the skill God imparts often comes the desire to do the very thing we're good at. We do it, we like it, and we generally enjoy what we do.

Knowing our gifts allows us to not waste the skills or talents God has given us. Jesus makes clear the importance of using our God-given resources in the parable of the talents (Matt. 25:14–30). A man is going on a journey, but before leaving, he gives talents to several of his servants. The ancient unit of mass "talent" corresponds to 75 pounds, so a gold talent would be worth almost $1 million today. We're told these talents are given to each servant "according to his ability." Thus, the first is given five talents, the second receives two, and the third gets one talent. These are significant sums of money. Each is called to do his best with what he's been assigned.

When the man returns, he demands an accounting. The first two servants have dutifully invested the money in such a way that it's doubled. The reward of "well done, good and faithful servant" is given to both. The last servant buried his assets in the ground and only returned the single talent he'd been given. "You wicked, lazy servant!" the master scolds.

What is not tolerated is the failure to use the gifts given to him. The point Jesus is making is that we, too, are stewards of "talents" here on earth. They are of great value when applied and not wasted. And the rewards are commensurate with the use of these gifts for God's purposes. In God's eyes, whether we have one, two, or five talents, if we put them to work, the reward will be the same: "Well done, good and faithful servant."

Nothing we have done in the past is ever wasted, even those skills we developed before we began to follow Jesus. You may have been successful in your business career or had significant schooling in your area of expertise. Some feel that all those skills belong to their old way of living and should be left behind. Nothing could be further from what God has in mind. The apostle Paul's rabbinic training and Roman citizenship made it possible for him to fulfill God's call to establish churches all over the Mediterranean. Likewise, Moses was raised and educated by an Egyptian pharaoh, training that enabled him to confront Egypt's authorities and lead his people. When we come to God, we retain all the experience and abilities we had before. God calls us to pick up right where we are and figure out how we are to use our experience and abilities to make a difference in the world for him.

An understanding of the talents and abilities God has given us is essential to knowing what we should be doing. You've probably known someone who was really good at something but wanted to follow another pursuit, something that was hardly a fit with his or her skills or gifts. After speaking at various conferences, I've had people come up to me and explain their career plans. Sometimes their intended pursuits seem obviously incongruent with their skills or gifts. Perhaps the manager who wants to go off and become an entrepreneur—or vice versa. Managerial and entrepreneurial skills are very different, yet that fact is often lost on those contemplating the transition from one to the other. We are each endowed with skills and abilities, and we must understand what those gifts are—and then apply them.

God rarely calls people out of their giftings; he calls us to fulfill our giftings. We need to learn and understand our gifts in order to discern our mission.

Create a Mission Statement

I was recently teaching on Acts 26:16–18, where Paul recounts how Jesus gave him his life mission. I emphasized the importance of a personal mission statement, a clear statement of what you feel God has called you to do. One of the group members made a very profound comment. "I have been in business many years, and I've never started any project or venture without having a clear mission and objectives statement," he explained. "I wouldn't even dream of starting anything without one, and yet I have never thought about creating one for my life. I am not sure why." Many of us have likewise never even considered it. And often when we do, something stops us from following through.

When I first heard this advice regarding a mission statement some 30 years ago, I approached the issue with some apprehension. I remember taking a blank piece of paper out of my desk at work and praying about my own statement. After titling the page "Life Goals," I sat there and stared at it for a while. Nothing came to me. Finally, I wrote a single point and let it sit. Then I added another point. It took several more days before I was satisfied, and then I put it away. A while later I pulled it out to review. Here's what I came up with:

Life Goals
1. *To be a witness to my employees.*
2. *To be a witness to the business community.*
3. *To provide funding to Christian work around the world—to leverage the work of the gospel.*

Writing a set of objectives isn't easy. What if it's wrong? Pray that God will lead you in creating it. And do not fear that it is cast in cement and unchangeable. You may end up modifying your statement as the Lord gives you insight into what he has for you. Believe that God will help you put it together and redirect you if necessary. It's comforting to know the document you write may not be the last word.

The most important thing is to get started from where you are. Avoid complex, detailed mission statements in which you get lost. It should be like a business mission statement that is powerful only in its focus and simplicity. By limiting the number of points, you will more easily keep sight of them. I have found a statement of one to three points to be memorable and regularly reviewable.

My mission statement includes being a witness to my employees and to the business community (by word and deed; all has to be pleasing to God) and to fund Christian work around the world. At the time I wrote it, this mission statement seemed a bit audacious. I had a fledgling company with a few employees and was pretty much unknown in the business community. I certainly did not have much money with which to fund Christian work. But even though I wasn't sure *how* the mission God gave would be fulfilled, I always trusted he would redirect me to the *what* (the right objectives) if a change was necessary.

As audacious as mine seemed at the time, it has not changed much since I wrote it. But I am amazed at how the focus and the tactics have shifted over the years. For example, there was a period when I ran a company and had more employees than money. My focus was on the first two objectives, to be a witness to my employees and to the business community. I shared through meetings, company newsletters, statements in my office. I also sought to pursue company values, personal interactions, and service qualities that reflected my commitment to follow Jesus. As our company grew and became noticed, I was asked to speak to various business groups. I had a successful platform from which I could tell my faith story.

Later, I experienced a shift. I now have few employees with whom I can share, but much of my time is spent sharing with the business community and supporting kingdom work around the world. In order to provide funding to Christian work, my wife and I created Living Stones Foundation. As a witness to the extended business community, I have been involved in the writing of three books, the proceeds of which go to our foundation. I look at my life goals even today and see no reason to change them.

When Good Is the Enemy of Great

Often we're asked to do things that are nice and helpful but do not fit our mission. We're inclined to respond positively out of guilt or a feeling of responsibility. Compounding the issue, many of us have a tendency to confuse a need we *could* meet with a need we *should* meet—our calling. Oswald Chambers states it succinctly: "The need is not the call." And more than likely, our calling does not involve spending our time doing things we don't do well.

Many years ago, a friend at church who was leaving the area asked me to pick up his ministry service. Being a young Christian, I felt guilty and obligated, even though the assignment didn't really fit me or my interests. Over the next two years I struggled mightily with it, burning myself out trying to accomplish what he'd been able to do so easily. I ultimately realized what I had to offer was not what was really needed in this situation, and I resigned the work, exhausted and disappointed. Since I wasn't clear on my gifts and calling, I failed to recognize that this assignment wasn't for me.

By filling a need that's outside our calling, we're doing what someone else is called to do. We end up working on good projects, but they're ones God never intended for us, and they keep us from accomplishing what we should have done. Doing the good prevents us from doing the great.

When you have a clear picture of your mission and goals, you can more comfortably say "no" to things that are not part of your mission, things that can and will overload you. Hanging on the cross, Jesus stated, "It is finished." There remained millions of needs all over the world, yet he proclaimed his work done. That's because he knew his mission, what he was called to do, and he kept himself to that mission.

It is important to review your mission statement from time to time, perhaps mentally, and compare it with what you're actually doing. These are the times for reflection and prayer. Are you still on target, doing the things on your mission statement? Is God leading you to modify some aspect of it? There are thousands of things you *can* do, and yet there are specific things to which God is *calling* you. Sorting them out is one of the most valuable exercises you can do in your life.

How You Work: Transform It with Seven Truths

If we're going to increase the spiritual impact of our work itself, we need to have a noble view of the work we do. Let's look at seven truths about our work that can elevate it from the mundane to the pursuit of a sacred calling. Without the right perception of our work, we will not perform it with excellence, and the spiritual impact of our work will be lacking.

1. Ours Jobs Are a Gift from God

We need to start by thanking God for the jobs we have. I witness too many followers of Jesus who spend their life complaining about work. As a result, they're not positive or contagious. Our jobs may not be everything that we desire or envision, but approached with a right attitude and goal, work is a sacred activity where we have the opportunity to minister to others and bring glory to God through faithful service. So we need to thank God for the work he has provided.

In my travels, I've had a chance to meet missionaries stationed all over the world. When I ask them what are the highest-priority needs in their communities, "jobs" usually ranks among the top two items listed and rarely lower than number three. The unemployment rate greatly exceeds 50 percent in some developing nations. Without work, people would be unable to have even the basic necessities. Sometimes it's important to be thankful that we even have a job at all.

We also need to thank him for what we are to learn at work. We must thank him for the lives we are to affect. We are thankful because in our work there is meaning and purpose. A thankful heart is the beginning of a new attitude, a positive attitude that gives us the ability to see our world quite differently than when we are disgruntled. With a thankful heart we are open to learning new things. We are willing to go the extra mile. We are able to see our work for what it is—a gift from God that demands our gratitude and our best effort. Our challenge is to use that gift to maximize God's glory.

2. God Shapes Us through Our Work

The work God has given each of us is no accident. Whether we like our jobs or not, God has placed us there for the purpose of continuing the work he's started in our lives. He may be using the work to teach us new skills, improve an area with which we have difficulty, or provide us the experience required for the next event. He may be using the job to prepare us for something bigger. He uses everything in our lives to prepare us for our ultimate destination—to be conformed to his Son and join him in heaven.

You may recall the 1984 film *The Karate Kid*. It's the story of Daniel, a youngster who is new in town and bullied by a larger boy. He befriends Mr. Miyagi, the handyman in his apartment building who promises to teach him the craft of martial arts. Daniel is eager to learn moves that will fell his foe, but the old master starts by handing him a rag and instructing the youngster to wash his car. "Wax on, wax off," says Mr. Miyagi as he demonstrates the sweeping motion used to clean the vehicle. The young man is furious and initially refuses to do the work. He's oblivious to the fact that the exercise is really teaching him a motion he will desperately need to perfect in order to become an expert karate fighter. Daniel doesn't see the connection between the work he is doing and the objectives the master has in mind. So the boy feels he is being used. Eventually he washes the car halfheartedly, feeling more sorry for himself than eager to perform the work. He is frustrated by what appears to be a lack of progress toward his goal.

How often have we felt that way? We feel underutilized. We consider our work boring and demeaning. We are convinced we're better than what we're doing. We think of our work as lacking real significance or spiritual value. As a result, we give our work very little thought and effort. We consider our jobs places where we do our time and earn the money to afford what we really enjoy. Has it occurred to you that God has a purpose for what we're doing at our work?

In *The Karate Kid*, the master becomes angry with the boy for his lackadaisical attitude. "You're free to quit," Mr. Miyagi rants, "but if I'm going to teach you, it's my way or not at all." Daniel isn't a happy camper, but he finally decides to do as the master asks. Later, when the boy has performed the waxing motion ad nauseam and can do it in his sleep, Mr. Miyagi shows him the utility of the exercise. Daniel realizes he's been learning the motions needed to become an expert in his field. Wanting his student to have no preconceived notions about the movement, the master had not explained the meaning of the exercise at the outset.

God is often like that with us. The Master does not always tell us why we are doing what we are doing. He calls us simply to be obedient and do whatever task is given to us to the best of our abilities. Therefore, it's important for us to approach whatever job we have with the right attitude. The right attitude helps to reduce our fatigue and keeps us from burning out. It shapes our thinking and allows us to be renewed. It keeps us from struggling against what God is attempting to do in our lives.

3. We Are Called to Difficult Work

Some have a strange view that life becomes easy once one commits to following Jesus. Indeed, there are many promises of blessings for those who seek first God's kingdom. Some are described in this chapter. But stopping there is simplistic and naïve—and it misses a richer reality. "In this world you will have trouble," Jesus promised (John 16:33). That includes the realm of work. When Adam was kicked out of the garden, he was told he would work by the sweat of his brow. That rule has never changed. We are called to work that is sometimes very hard. We are called to situations that are sometimes very messy.

We are also called to approach business in a manner that runs contrary to conventional thought, and in the process we'll encounter disagreement. Sometimes we will find ourselves alone. Many a time, I came home from work feeling beat up and abused. I felt like the only one who was committed to a principle. When people thought I was out of step with reality, my wife, Roberta, would pick me up, encourage me, and then send me back the next day to face many tough issues. God was always faithful in times of trouble to provide the necessary support. Our work will be difficult, but he is willing to help. He has promised to walk though the tough times with us.

4. We Are Called to Work Hard

I have seen some Christians who go to work to talk about their faith but view their "secular" tasks as unimportant and not worth the effort. As a result, they'll give less than a 100-percent effort to their employer. This is not God's plan. "All hard work brings a profit, but mere talk leads only to poverty," Scripture tells us (Prov. 14:23). It always amazes me when I see people who go through life putting in a 90 percent effort when with just marginally more work, they could be superior stars in the field of their endeavor. Thomas Sowell puts it this way: "Doing 90 percent of what is required is one of the biggest wastes because you have nothing to show for all your efforts. But doing 110 percent of what is expected is one of the smartest investments because it can pay off with a big reputation for just a little more effort."[73]

The small difference in effort makes a world of difference to those around us, to our potential, and to our ability to influence others. As Christians, we should be the example of those who work harder. We should support our company and co-workers with vigor. We should serve customers to the best of our abilities. We are called to work hard, because it's an important part of our ministry.

Some Christians have the impression they just need to show up at work and God will do the rest. Yes, God will do his part—but he has gifted and called us to do ours! Some equate working hard with worrying about material possessions. But work is not worry; they are very different. While worry may indeed drive some to work hard, that doesn't invalidate giving a full effort in our jobs. It simply invalidates worry as the motive for our effort. Our diligent work is truly noble when it springs from a desire to serve customers, colleagues, and employers in the best way possible.

5. We Work to Serve Others to God's Glory

We have seen business is not simply about maximizing profit, as many management experts would have us believe. At its core, our goal in business is to bring glory to God through service to others. We are to serve people as if we're serving God himself (Eph. 6:7).

Bob Dylan's song "Gotta Serve Somebody" makes the point that everyone serves others. No matter what our station in life, he notes, we're obligated to someone else:

You may be a businessman or some high degree thief,
They may call you Doctor or they may call you Chief,
But you're gonna have to serve somebody, yes indeed,
You're gonna have to serve somebody,
Well, it may be the devil or it may be the Lord,
But you're gonna have to serve somebody.

Dylan also recognizes that we're serving both on a human and on a spiritual level. In our work, we should be in service to others and to God. Jesus told us he came to serve; we can do no less. Whether it's a customer or a colleague, our job is to serve him or her to the glory of God.

Our model is Jesus. He called us to be servants to others. Though it usually goes by different names, the concept of servant leadership is beginning to catch on, even in secular business education. How does a servant manager operate? Such a manager focuses on others, walks humbly, recognizes the gifting in others, and brings out the best in his or her employees. Rather than lording it over others, a servant leader identifies needs and looks for ways to serve and support.

For those who don't manage others, their emphasis should be on helping the boss and peers succeed—or even offer to take on extra work to help lighten another's load. Imagine approaching the boss and asking what you might do to make his or her goals easier to obtain. As a co-worker, you might plan to spend some time after work to help a struggling employee. This love in action presents the gospel in a powerful way.

I should also note that serving our employer or investor means that we'll work so that our product is more valuable than the cost of the product. For those of us selling goods or services, the application is obvious. We will be able to continue serving others if the sales price or value exceeds our cost. But what about those of us who answer phones or manage the assembly line? How does the profit component apply to those jobs? Quite simply, each of us is a profit center. We're "earning a profit" if we're more valuable than we cost. In other words, we will be able to continue serving others if our employer considers our contribution worth more than our salary. We work to serve others to God's glory, and a profit is necessary in order to continue serving people.

You may recall the opening of Inmac's Scottish manufacturing plant when our new employees were concerned about our commitment to the facility (Chapter 4). How long would we keep this plant? they wanted to know. The plant would remain viable, stated our VP of Human Relations Al Cotton, as long as it produced products that were competitive with those anywhere else in the world. Unless we're cost-effective, we cannot continue to serve others.

6. We Point Others to God Through Our Work

Jesus said, "Let your light shine before men, that they may see your good deeds and praise your Father in heaven" (Matt. 5:16). Rather than hide our light under a bushel basket, we're told to let it shine brightly for all to see. Our purpose is to be light to the world, and it's the bright light of our "good deeds" that points others to God. What is the implication for our work? It's that the quality of our work and the sincerity of our personal interactions in the work environment can be a bright light to those who are exposed to us at work. (But if there's nothing exemplary about our work, the light shines only dimly.) If we're called to business, demonstrating the gospel through our work is an important part of our ministry.

"Preach the gospel at all times. If necessary, use words," St. Francis of Assisi once said. The demonstration of the gospel is the most important form of preaching, and I can think of no venue better suited to it than the business world. Where else can people observe followers of Jesus on a daily basis as they exhibit God's love and follow his principles in good times and bad? I can assure you that God's people working in vocational Christian professions are positioned much less advantageously in this regard than his followers working in the marketplace. And when we faithfully demonstrate the gospel by deed, we point others to Jesus and have opportunities to share the gospel by word.

7. Our Work Has Spiritual Value

As we described in Chapter 8, those of us who are followers of Jesus are sometimes inclined to discount our "secular" work as lacking and inferior. Perhaps we consider our work's only redemptive aspects to be the opportunity to share our faith with others and the income it provides to support ministries. But make no mistake: when done with the proper direction, our work in the world most definitely has spiritual value.

The spiritual value of our work lies in its success in advancing God's own goals, in helping further his purpose through service and creation. In this way our daily work is our spiritual act of worship. John Stott writes that "work is worship, provided we can see how our job contributes, in however small and indirect a way, to the forwarding of God's plan for mankind."[74] Making the connection between our work in the marketplace and God's larger purposes is not always easy or obvious. It may require a bit of reflection on what God's doing in the world.

Take some time to think about the spiritual value of your work—what you do and how you do it. I've found the following considerations from Alistair Mackenzie and Wayne Kirkland helpful. In your work, how can you (among other things):[75]

- Serve others with joy
- Steward resources well
- Employ God-given creativity
- Be truthful and encourage such habits as honesty and integrity
- Bring healing, understanding, and reconciliation
- Build community, and promote peace and harmony
- Nurture and encourage others' gifts and character development
- Witness to God's truth

As you do these things, you will clearly advance God's kingdom.

This chapter described how to improve our ministry *of* work—how we can increase the spiritual impact of the work we do and how we do it. You may also find a couple of additional real-life examples helpful in the process of realizing deeper integration in your own life. In the next chapter, we'll look at some individuals who decided their faith needed to have a profound impact on their work. They represent explosive examples of living the integrated business life where several of the principles we've outlined are working together in a single individual. Some of their actions and results will astound you. And they will certainly encourage you to think outside the box of conventional, everyday business.

PART V

Living the
Integrated Business Life

To kick off this concluding Part, let's recap where we've been. We started our journey by describing the workplace forces and internal tensions that lead us to compartmentalize our lives by segregating work, faith, and family. (Part I) We then examined and corrected some misguided beliefs and attitudes that stem from our business education (Part II) and church teaching (Part III) and serve to compound the problem of separating our faith and work. Then we learned how to achieve greater integration by partnering with God and increasing the spiritual impact of our work life ministry. (Part IV)

God's plan is for us to live integrated, abundant lives. We can certainly learn from examples of other believers in a variety of situations who have found deeper integration of their faith and work. (Chapter 13) And when we live more integrated lives and impact the marketplace, we will start to see transformation in the places where we walk in integrity. (Chapter 14) But what's needed to make the breakthrough to integrated living in our own lives? (Chapter 15) Let's see.

CHAPTER 13

The Shepherd of the Ritz

To glorify God as we supply our customers worldwide with top quality, value-priced batteries, related electrical power-source products, and distribution services.

(Interstate Batteries mission statement)

The fantastic growth of Buck Knives was no accident. From the beginning, management determined to make God the Senior Partner. In a crisis, the problem was turned over to Him, and He hasn't failed to help us with the answer.

(Al Buck, Founder, Buck Knives)

To honor God in all that we do by respecting others, by doing good work, by helping others, by forgiving others, by giving thanks, by celebrating our lives.

(Dacor company values)

Stories of Integration

There is no single picture of *the* integrated life. But many have struggled with the challenge of finding greater integration between their faith and their work, and there's something we can learn from their experiences and successes. This chapter highlights several individuals in diverse industries and vastly different positions who have found new paradigms for their roles in the marketplace. They have discovered and adopted ways of better integrating their work and their faith and attributing greater meaning to their vocation. They have increased the spiritual impact of their work lives. These are their stories.

Johnny the Bagger

One need not have a lofty position in the corporation to minister to others through service. No matter where one sits on the organizational chart, when customers and co-workers see the fruit of the Spirit at work, the business environment becomes ripe for transformation. Selfless service can be infectious! Perhaps the most inspirational example of this is the story of Johnny the Bagger.[76]

Several years ago, a large supermarket chain brought in a professional speaker to address 3,000 of its frontline service people about something it deeply desired: building customer loyalty. A large collection of cashiers, baggers, produce people, floral specialists, butchers, bakers, stockers, and truck drivers listened as the presenter issued a challenge. "Every one of you can make a difference and create meaningful memories for your customers that will motivate them to come back. How?" she asked, letting the question hang in the room. "Go home tonight and think about something you can do for your customers to make them feel special—a memory that will make them want to come back and shop at your store again."

In the audience sat a young man named Johnny. He was a nineteen-year-old bagger at one of the supermarket chain's stores. Johnny also had Down syndrome. He liked the speaker's idea but couldn't think of anything special he could do for his store's customers. *How can I make a difference in the lives of those I encounter every day at work?* Johnny thought. *After all, I'm just a bagger.*

Then he had an idea. Every night after work, he found a Thought for the Day. And if he couldn't find one he liked, he'd think one up! Once a good saying had been located, his dad helped him reproduce it six times on a page and print fifty copies. Johnny dutifully cut each page into slips of paper with the quote and signed his name to the back. (Note the extra hours spent on his work to serve others—he was leveraging his time at work.) He came equipped to work the next day with a brown bag full of sayings.

The stash of quotes next to him, Johnny would finish each customer's bagging by placing a copy of the saying in the bag. "Thanks for shopping with us," he'd say with a smile. Though many would consider his a thankless and unimportant job with little redeeming value, Johnny had made his work important and precious. He was loving and serving customers. He was ministering to people.

Several weeks later, the store manager was making his rounds and discovered that the line at one of the checkouts was three times longer than at any of the others. It was Johnny's lane. Concerned that there was something amiss and that Johnny needed help, he summoned all available cashiers to the front of the store to open additional lanes. The store manager then prompted those waiting in line at Johnny's checkout to switch to a newly opened one. But to his surprise nobody would move! "No, it's okay," they responded. "We want to be in Johnny's lane. We want his Thought for the Day." Wow! One woman approached the manager and excitedly grabbed his arm. "I used to shop at your store only once a week," she explained. "But now I come in every time I go by, because I want to get Johnny's Thought for the Day."

Without question, this young bagger had become the most important person in the store. But his influence reached well beyond the customers he touched. Others working in the supermarket took notice, and Johnny's example transformed the store. The floral department discovered a wonderful use for broken flowers and unused corsages. Instead of discarding them, the floral specialists would take the flowers out onto the supermarket floor to find an elderly woman or young girl on whom to pin them. A butcher bought thousands of Snoopy stickers. When wrapping a piece of meat, he'd stick his favorite character on it. Every cashier started adding his or her personal signature as well, creating memories for their customers. They began to see their work as more than just a job.

As the spirit of service spread throughout the store, it created a buzz. Customers started talking about the supermarket. They came back—and brought their friends. "Aim for service, and success will follow," declared Albert Schweitzer. I think those front-line service workers can attest to that.

We can transform the marketplace no matter how much organizational power our positions grant us. One youngster with Down syndrome made it his mission to make a difference and really serve people. How can you transform the way you approach, perform, and think about your work? Perhaps, like Johnny, you could use a new paradigm for business that gives it greater spiritual value and meaning. When we truly love and serve others to the glory of God, our work has spiritual value beyond what we could have imagined. And as we'll see next, our job becomes our ministry to others.

The Shepherd of the Ritz

Recently, my wife Roberta and I had the privilege of visiting Washington DC for a series of events. We stayed at one of the nicest hotels in town, the Ritz Carlton. Customer service is Ritz Carlton's hallmark, and as one might expect, the service at their hotel in the nation's capital is impeccable. Guests are greeted as if they're visiting potentates. It takes a lot of work to get a hospitality team so involved with the many guests who come and go. Perhaps a little undersized for the number of rooms at the hotel, the lobby was constantly busy.

The hotel was staffed with bellboys, concierges, registration clerks, and account settlement staff. There were also one or two people who appeared to be greeters. Strategically located between the entrance and the elevators, they had a clear view of both areas. One particular gentleman always had a smile, making eye contact with the guests as he greeted them. He was there at the door with a kind word as we left in the evening and again as we returned later at night.

His had the makings of a very tedious job with very little to show for his work. He didn't seem to be making or producing anything. The job required standing near the entrance for hours—uncomfortable and cold on those January days. And with so many guest encounters, his chances of picking up a sickness must have been a valid concern. I suspect many of us would lapse into depression over a job we consider tedious and of little value. But I noticed that despite all the reasons he might feel that way, this man seemed to enjoy himself and take his work quite seriously. It made me curious.

One evening, Roberta and I were returning from an event. We'd seen this man when we left the hotel. "Hello," he'd said with a nod, a warm tone of recognition in his voice and expression. "Have a nice evening!" Now he was there to greet us when we returned to the hotel. It was late, and we were both tired from a long evening. But he seemed as fresh as when we'd left. We were hurrying to catch an elevator when he extended a greeting.

As we hopped in, my wife playfully asked, "Did you miss us?"

His response almost stopped Roberta in her tracks. In the friendliest manner and with a big smile, he said, "I have been praying for you all the time you were gone."

I didn't hear the comment, as it was directed just to her, but on the ascent to our floor she told me what he'd said. I wasn't sure what he'd meant, but I was intrigued and wanted to ask him. We got off at our floor and called the elevator to take us right back down.

At that time of night the place was not very crowded. The greeter was there, and we asked to speak with him. "What did you mean by that comment about praying for us while we were gone?" I asked.

With the same warm smile he began to tell us that God had given him this job at the Ritz Carlton. His responsibilities were to greet guests and to provide for their security by making sure no unauthorized persons went up to the guest room areas. In this job, he explained, he could pray for everyone coming in or out of the hotel. "So I was praying for you while you were gone," he concluded.

I stood there amazed, realizing this man was much more than a security guard and greeter. He viewed his work as more meaningful than observing the people who came in, interacting with guests, and protecting them from harm. He considered the guests as the flock that God had entrusted to him. He saw himself as one who needed to lift them up in prayer and thus fulfill God's commandment to love each other, to help each other without strings attached. He saw himself as partnering with God to be God's man among those put in front of him. He saw his job as a ministry that God had given him.

As I reflect back on this man and his attitude toward his daily work, several important points come to mind. First, his story illustrates very clearly how one can integrate one's business and spiritual life within the boundaries of the workday. (Integration of faith and work need not add hours at work.) He found a way to make his current job a ministry, not augment his workday with some ministry event or activity that further burdened his schedule. God may be leading some to start a prayer group in the office, but unless we recognize and treat our work itself as a ministry a calling, we'll remain conflicted about the ultimate value of our everyday tasks. And that's where we spend the bulk of our time and energy.

Second, a significant part of this man's ministry was done in silence. Sure, his ministry included outward service to others by smiling, greeting, and protecting. But he was also serving them through prayer, and while that was done without public acknowledgement, God was certainly pleased and glorified. God was watching and listening.

While at school at Auburn University, my son Justin felt called by God to get dressed up one morning and go down to the area reserved on campus for public speaking. There, God called him to share the good news. With the Bible in one hand, he steeled up his nerves and began to speak. As time went by, no one seemed to stop to listen. Sadly, he said to the Lord, "No one is listening." He heard the Lord reply, "I'm listening." Others may not always recognize our work, but we know that the Lord is watching and listening. We're simply called to be faithful and to glorify God in whatever situation he has placed us—even if the personal value does not always seem apparent.

Third, this man demonstrated that any believer in the marketplace can embody an integrated life. One need not have a position of leadership, power, or prestige to integrate one's faith and work. As what might be considered a lowly greeter and security guard, this man recognized how his work had significant spiritual value and discovered how he could further serve those he encountered in the course of his work. He performed his assigned duties with excellence. And he went beyond the service required of his position by committing the hotel's guests to prayer. His ministry was serving guests of the hotel to the glory of God.

As we finished our conversation, my wife Roberta suggested to the man, "Then you are God's shepherd."

His eyes widened and reflected a sudden insight. A huge smile came across his face. "I guess I am," he replied humbly. "I guess I'm the Shepherd of the Ritz!"

God's Business

There are other good examples of business people who see their work as ministry and seek to further God's kingdom through it. My friend Paul Schaller is using his business education and experience to run a unique company that's supporting missionary aviation. In 1995, he pursued his passion for flying and earned a pilot's license. Paul's a graduate of M.I.T.'s business school and has a lengthy track record of guiding Silicon Valley startup companies. He started consulting in the non-profit area and spent some time working at his church. God would weave together Paul's business experience, non-profit background, and personal hobby at a company called Quest Aircraft.

An aircraft designer and a missionary aviation pilot founded Quest in 1999. These men sought to produce a different type of aircraft, one required by missionary pilots flying non-profit staff and supplies to remote locations around the world. Traditional aircraft companies focused on corporate jets or small aircraft. Neither was ideal for missionary aviation.

Quest's plane accommodates large payloads and short runways. It runs on jet fuel, which is typically used by commercial and military aviation and thus more widely available in remote locations than aviation gas. Quest discovered that this type of aircraft also has plenty of commercial demand. When its KODIAK plane received FAA certification in 2007, commercial orders were backlogged nearly three years.

The plane is bringing missionary aviation into the 21st century by replacing the older models being flown in the field. Mission Aviation Fellowship is replacing Cessna 206s with KODIAK planes that can carry nearly twice the cargo. That means it's cutting in half the cost per cargo pound.

Quest Aircraft is a for-profit company that truly partners with mission agencies. In fact, mission groups are both "investors" and customers. The company's initial funding came in the form of deposits on aircraft from non-profit mission agencies—an innovative, unique funding scheme. Quest also provides planes to mission organizations at a significant discount from the commercial price. The "one-in-ten program" is designed to deliver one discounted aircraft to missionary pilots for every nine sold to commercial outfits. Quest even raises some of the funds the mission groups need to pay for the new planes. And the company intends to support missionary work through its corporate profits as well. "We set up the company to last in perpetuity to serve missionary aviation," says Paul Schaller.

Paul first joined Quest's board and then became CEO in 2004. The company's novel funding structure was derived from years of experience helping people start companies. Most in the senior management team share Paul's faith and commitment to support missionary aviation. Prospective employees are told about the company's purpose; some who are marginal Christians or atheists have become followers of Jesus as a result of their involvement with Quest. Commercial customers have expressed a fondness for the company's social values bent. Vendors are also generally enthusiastic about Quest's objectives, and some suppliers have even volunteered to give the tenth item free. Paul concludes, "Running a company that has an overriding purpose is really rewarding!"[77]

Quest Aircraft has made such a stir in the aviation industry that Paul has received feelers from others interested in purchasing the company. His reply has stunned a number of would-be buyers. "I can't sell the business," he tells them. "Only God owns the company."

Business as Mission: The Purposeful Business of Transforming Communities

As business people begin to integrate their faith and work and realize that their work in the marketplace is their ministry, a growing number are taking the concept further—literally to the ends of the earth! Inspired by their faith and desiring to serve and bless people all over the world, talented entrepreneurs are establishing "kingdom businesses" in developing nations. They're seeking to minister to people in other cultures through business, with the goal of furthering economic and spiritual transformation in countries that desperately need it. (My earlier book *God Is at Work: Transforming People and Nations Through Business* is a thorough presentation of the objectives and approaches of those doing "business as mission.")

My friend Clem Schultz is one such kingdom entrepreneur who has found a remarkable way of integrating his faith and business overseas. He's an American MBA who was a divisional manager in China for a large multinational company. He also possesses both an enormous entrepreneurial drive and a heart for blessing the Chinese through business.

In 1989, Clem acquired AMI (both are pseudonyms) and has guided the company since then in the establishment and operation of top-notch manufacturing and media facilities in China.[78] AMI's client list includes household names, large corporations that seek expertise in navigating the complex process of establishing factories in China. On behalf of their clients, Clem and his team perform feasibility studies, research the market, select the location, handle licensing and registration, acquire and import equipment, and hire and manage manufacturing staff. AMI often takes minority equity stakes in the $1–$10 million facilities it builds and manages.

Since a breakthrough $3 million lighting manufacturing deal in 1990, AMI has helped start or grow more than 40 factories, with AMI providing an equity investment in 15 of those ventures. As of 2007, there were ten factories or media businesses in which AMI continued its equity or management involvement. These businesses provide jobs for more than 1,000 Chinese nationals and generate in excess of $50 million in revenue per year.

AMI's mission statement reads: "To start and grow world-class business operations on behalf of our U.S.A.-based holding company and our multinational clients, and to recruit and train our management and investor teams around a common shared set of Christian values and ethics." Clem's staff includes professionals from the United States, England, Malaysia, New Zealand, South America, and elsewhere who share his faith and his desire to transform people and nations through business. Most have been living in East Asia for years and have developed a keen understanding of the local environment. They realize that both the culture and business practices need to be redeemed.

As they manage new manufacturing facilities, AMI professionals are tasked with dual spiritual and profit objectives. In keeping with these two goals, the venture pursues both an evangelistic "Great Commission" plan and a business plan. Each company's CEO is accountable to two boards, one focused on the spiritual objectives and one focused on the economic objectives. Both boards have the authority to fire the leader if warranted, which serves to keep the organization's eye on achieving business results as well as spiritual transformation. Clem's "kingdom business" model represents a deep integration of faith and business at the personal and organizational level.

Here's an example of AMI's approach to combining business and faith objectives. Clem himself managed the construction and staffing of a Chinese manufacturing subsidiary of a multinational corporation based in the United States. Within one year he built a factory with 500 employees, $34 million in annual sales, and an Arthur Andersen award for "overall best manufacturing startup in China." But while growing the company, Clem was equally focused on developing followers of Jesus. He understood that successful business principles come from the Bible, so as part of a formal training program on business ethics, employees were taught and asked to internalize business principles based on biblical values. Christian staff modeled these values as well, declaring the message of Jesus by word and by deed. On average, ten employees came to faith each month. In a five-month period, four new house churches formed.

"Our large-dollar and high-technology amounts of investment provide us with strong political leverage with governments," Clem explains. "East Asian governments generally welcome foreign manufacturers, especially those with fairly large capitalization. As long as a company makes money and provides jobs for the local people, the governments will not interfere—unless it is rather openly breaking the law." Clem has leveraged his political favor in the areas where AMI operates manufacturing facilities to help bring more than twenty nonprofit partner organizations to the regions. These strategic allies have no financial ties to AMI, but they do share the company's desire to bless the local communities through education, development, and church planting.

Individuals and organizations whose objectives are purely evangelistic in nature have approached Clem with the request to accommodate them within one of his businesses. Often they'll have notions of using "employment" at the company as a cover for their church work. Clem sometimes grants such employment requests, but only on the condition that the job is performed with full sincerity. He expects an honest day's work from everyone; there is no special exemption for those who consider their true calling something more spiritual apart from the business. In fact, he prohibits evangelism during business hours. A firm believer in the principle of earning the right to be heard, Clem considers exceptional, selfless service to customers and fellow employees—in other words, sharing the gospel by deed—the foundation from which to share one's faith by word. Thus, evangelism objectives cannot justify neglecting one's duties and stealing work hours from one's employer.

As inspirational as Clem's story is to those of us seeking models for an integrated life, I should issue a word of caution to those itching to buy a ticket to China, India, or Africa. Unless you've achieved some level of integration in your own culture, you will find it even more challenging to do so in a foreign environment. So start by determining how you can increase the spiritual impact of your current work and how you can better serve others to the glory of God in your current marketplace. It may require thinking outside the box.

Thinking Outside the Box to Get to the Heart of the Matter

I was recently advising an Internet entrepreneur whose company was growing and appeared to have a great future. But his fellow investors had lost interest, and he wanted to buy them out. His question was how to raise the money in order to get full control of the company. Since he already owned more than 50 percent of the company, I stopped him at this point and asked why he needed to get full ownership? "My church is buying real estate in Central America to provide small plots to local farmers," he explained. "It'll enable them to make a living." The economic development effort was part of a program to spread the gospel overseas, and he wanted to provide funds from the company over the long term for this project. He also felt his present partners wouldn't share his desire to spend the company's earning this way.

"What do you know about agriculture or real estate investing in Central America?" I asked him.

"Nothing," was the reply.

"Then why would you take your income and skills and apply them to a field about which you know nothing?"

"Well, my church is doing it," he stated.

"What does your church know about agriculture or real estate in Central America?" Turned out, they knew very little.

"What if you used your company to help these same people in Central America?" I asked. "As a retail Internet merchant, consider using your selling power and the power of the Internet business to open an operation in Central America that would provide jobs to those in need. You could weave a great story into your promotion, advance the sales of these products, and give those folks the jobs they desperately need—and satisfy your investors in the process." It was an "aha" moment for him.

Sometimes we need to think outside the box and get away from convention to see the very opportunities God has put in front of us. God has put us where we are for a specific purpose. Whether this was my friend's purpose or not, it started him thinking in a new direction, as he realized the possibility of powerfully integrating business and spiritual objectives.

Glorifying God in Business

Our business takes on new meaning and purpose when we realize we can glorify God in our work life, when we view our work as our ministry. It doesn't matter whether you are an owner of a business, a manager in a business, or an employee.

Whether you lead one of the largest retailing corporations in the world or greet people in a hotel lobby, you can find ways to more effectively integrate your faith with your work. The process of transforming business starts with one person who is committed to making a difference, who is willing to be obedient to God and include him in his or her work.

I trust these short but diverse stories have inspired you to consider how you might transform your daily business into a place where your faith is at work—into a ministry that glorifies God! One common theme in all these stories of integration is a bold willingness to allow faith to permeate one's work. If we are to do likewise, we need to convert from thermometers to thermostats. What does that mean? I'll explain.

CHAPTER 14

Transforming the Marketplace

[One] of the major weaknesses of Christianity ... is the tendency to departmentalize our lives and confine the spiritual to its own little watertight compartment instead of letting it out to invade and transform the secular.

(Arthur Wallis, author, theologian)

You are the light of the world ... let your light shine before men, that they may see your good deeds and praise your Father in heaven.

(Jesus Christ, Matthew 5:14–16)

Society can change and must change one person at a time.

(George W. Bush,
43rd President of the United States)

Are You a Thermometer or a Thermostat?

Seeking advice, a young Californian woman approached me after a conference. She worked for a foundation and had been enjoying her work. The foundation supported medical research in fighting disease, and she felt the work they were doing was very beneficial to society. But she was agonizing over a new direction the organization was taking, a path she considered incompatible with her Christian faith. The state of California had recently decided to fund embryonic stem cell research, and the foundation was planning to support this area of research. She didn't want to be associated with an activity that ran counter to her strong moral convictions.

I asked what she'd done about the issue to date. Since the foundation's plan was still in the discussion stages, so far she'd only considered her options. Would she be willing to state her position to the organization's leadership? Doing so carried the distinct possibility of being fired, she explained. And if the foundation did proceed with the plan to support embryonic stem cell research, she felt she'd have to leave the organization.

What a tough situation! But this young lady is not alone. I'd venture to say all followers of Jesus in the marketplace encounter situations in which their work and their faith appear to be on a collision path. How would you respond if you were this young woman? Would you be like a thermometer or like a thermostat?

A thermometer is a simple device that responds to the temperature around it. It is calibrated to an external standard so that its scale reflects the temperature it encounters. But a thermometer makes no evaluations and takes no action to affect the environment. If the temperature rises or drops, it simply records the event. It's a chameleon. It fits into its surroundings and participates regardless of the prevailing climate. In short, the thermometer records the temperature but has no impact on it.

In our compartmentalized lives, many of us have grown accustomed to operating like thermometers in the marketplace. We may note the temperature around us, but we do nothing to affect it. If the environment gets too crazy, we may decide our business situation and our faith are too incompatible to coexist. In those times of extreme temperatures, many of us conclude the only recourse is to leave or keep our mouths shut. But let me suggest another approach.

Like a thermometer, a thermostat also has a calibrated scale and displays the current temperature. But a thermostat is fundamentally different. When the temperature hits a certain point, it reacts in an effort to change the temperature. The thermostat in our house will trigger the heater when it's too cold and the air conditioner when it's too hot. The thermostat does not question the homeowner's settings. It doesn't question the outcome of the action it puts in motion or the results. It simply follows the orders of the owner.

Many of us need to learn to be like that thermostat at work. We must allow God's Word to give us a preset level at which we react to what's going on around us. If the standard of activity at work drops below God's accepted level, we must do more than note it—we must react and impact the environment. The environment change is not our responsibility, it's God's. The thermostat does not change the environment—the heater or air conditioner does. We are the little part that sets the bigger function in motion.

Being a thermostat means sticking out our necks and opening ourselves up to trouble. God doesn't always tell us what the specific outcome will be. Our only assurance is that we're being obedient to his voice. Being a thermostat means stepping out of our old compartments into an integrated life, and that can be frightening and uncharted territory for many of us.

Impacting People through Business

When we step into an integrated life to live as thermostats in the marketplace, God will use us to impact both people and business. We need to understand that business creates value, and believers in business have the opportunity to create value on both a physical and spiritual level. First, consider the fact that most economic transactions inherently create value. Why's that? If someone's willing to buy your product or service, it's more valuable to that person than the cash given in exchange. And to you the cash is worth more than the product or service, perhaps because it cost you less to produce it. That's how aggregate wealth is created and the standard of living is improved. So we create value just by transacting useful goods and services in an honest and transparent manner.

The second way the integrated Christian business life creates value is through the intangible aspects of a transaction. What I mean is the manner in which the interpersonal relationship plays out. It's how the fruit of the Spirit—love, joy, peace, patience, kindness, goodness, faithfulness, gentleness, self-control—is exhibited. It's the way a principled company takes care of its partners even when it's costly and the company's not legally required to do so. It's the way a customer is served beyond his expectations. It's the way the Shepherd of the Ritz smiles at guests, wishes them a good day, and prays for them while they're out. And it's the way a believer in business expresses the love of Jesus by word or by deed through his or her work. These are the qualities economists don't capture in their price versus quantity analyses, but they represent enormous value to individuals and to the marketplace.

Followers of Jesus in the marketplace are the hands and feet of God, the answer to Jesus' famous prayer "your kingdom come ... on earth as it is in heaven" (Matt. 6:10). We bring the kingdom via transactions, the simple building blocks of business. Why is the Lord interested in transactions? Aren't they secular in nature? Not in the least. The *process* of the transaction is the critical piece. Whether it involves an exchange of money or a commitment to do something for someone, each business interaction offers the opportunity to share God's love. These transactions should reflect "the ultimate transaction" which took place on the cross: the sacrifice of God's own Son on behalf of undeserving mankind in exchange for their salvation.

As we imitate the love of Jesus in our own transactions, we're a witness to the world. He can and will build his kingdom as spiritual capital is created and the marketplace is transformed one person at a time. And what we add to the spiritual bank account with each transaction can be used by the Holy Spirit to change the world.

Transforming the Marketplace

When our faith is integrated in such a way that it radically transforms the way we approach and conduct our work, it will impact our organizations and perhaps even change our industries. Those two merchants in the Middle Ages (Chapter 6) focused on the heart of business and acted on principle. They instituted business practices that glorified God and exhibited love for their neighbors. Before long, London's prevailing business customs had been transformed. Immoral dealings were replaced with transactions conducted with honest weights and measures. Two merchants resolved to redeem their own shops and ended up redeeming business in their time and place. Who knows where the Spirit of God will take our commitment when we're willing to step out and let our faith influence our work?

Several years ago, a friend asked for help in starting a company in his native India. It would be a call-center business that would take advantage of lower-cost, higher-skill labor and crystal-clear communication lines to serve American and multinational corporations. I agreed to help start the company, but only if the management would commit to hiring young Christians who were as qualified as the other applicants. (In India, there has been a lot of prejudice toward non-Hindu people, and employment can be a challenge for Christians.) I also asked them to give me time after hours and a place at work where I could provide Christian teaching to these young employees. The management readily agreed, and we set out to build ET into a world-class business.

Today, ET enjoys a great reputation, thanks to the highest-ranked service in the industry. We now have over 1,000 employees—primarily young, smart, college-educated professionals. A local Christian university has sent us excellent graduates, and 60 percent of the company calls itself Christian in a country where only 2 percent identify with the faith.

Like other call centers in India, we have a problem with high turnover. But the nature of our turnover is different. It's created by a demand for our employees, since we train them well and have a reputation for excellence. As a result, thousands of young Christian employees are working throughout the call center industry, having a significant impact as they deploy biblical work practices and share their faith with new colleagues. They are in a position to redeem their industry. It all started with a simple agreement to help a friend from an integrated Christian perspective.

... And Are of Like Mind

The transformation of London's business practices in the Middle Ages was started by a couple of merchants, and the evolving impact on India's call center industry was likewise set in motion by very few. It doesn't take many, but they must be like-minded. They must be on the same page.

I recall the day I approached my Inmac founding partner eager to tackle the task of designing our first product catalog.

"Before we start, I need you to read this," he said, handing me a copy of David Ogilvy's *Confessions of an Advertising Man*. This classic book by the father of modern advertising describes how to write potent copy and capture people's imagination.

After I studied Ogilvy's methods and devoured his advice, I went back to my partner. "Okay, I get it," I said. "Let's go." We were on the same page, ready to partner on the catalog content and design. When it came time to write the copy and do the layouts for our ultimately award-winning catalog, we were like-minded.

Perhaps you're sensing a desire to make a difference in your organization, industry, or sphere of influence. Remember that where two or more are gathered and are of like mind, there God will be ready to work (Matt. 18:19–20). I encourage you to find an accountability partner who's likewise committed to living an integrated life and seeing God transform the marketplace. And if you can't find someone who "gets it," approach another receptive heart in your circle and hand him or her a copy of this book. It's important to partner with someone who's on the same page.

A Witness to the World

The prosperity of redeemed business is a witness to the world. Two of my sons, Justin and Kary, joined me on a visit to a town in Guatemala that saw enormous revival. Thirty years ago, Almolonga was a place filled with bars and drunks sleeping in the streets. Almolonga's four jails and additional ones in neighboring towns were routinely filled with the town's unruly, disorderly, and inebriated residents. Then a very small group of believers prayed earnestly, and God started to transform the place. Today, more than 90 percent of the town is born again. The last jail was closed years ago. God redeemed their lackluster land, too, and the economy is thriving. Almolonga is now famous for yielding the most productive vegetable crop in Central America. The size of the vegetables they grow is simply astonishing! The carrots are as big as one's forearm yet sweet as baby ones.

We just had to bring some back so friends and family could witness God's miraculous blessings. As we passed through United States customs, we were reminded that our government doesn't permit travelers to bring fruits and vegetables into the country. So we presented the carrots and other giant vegetables in our possession to one of the agricultural border agents. His jaw dropped as he saw their size, and he wondered where these vegetables had originated. "They're from Almolonga, Guatemala," Justin replied, "from the town that prays." We had a short opportunity to recount God's spiritual and economic blessings on Almolonga.

He was about to confiscate our produce when another nearby agent appeared. He was aware of the Guatemalan town and came over to say, "It's okay. They can pass through. You'll find Almolonga in the book of acceptable produce."

"Oh, I've heard of the city," one of the agents chimed in. "They're Christians, aren't they?" This last remark started a conversation among the agents. As we scurried off with our oversized vegetables, we could hear the agent in the background continuing to explain God's miracles in that faithful town to his two intrigued and amazed associates. What a witness!

Does our work bear witness by transforming the marketplace? If not, how could it? How do we start down the path of integrated living? Venturing into the integrated business life might seem like a bold, risky move. But it's really not. It's breaking free from constraints that limit us. Let me explain.

CHAPTER 15

Venturing into the Integrated Business Life

If a man wants something he has never had before, he must do something he has never done before.

(Anonymous)

The abundant living that Jesus offers must be found in the pedestrian realities of Monday mornings, or not at all.

(Jedd Medefind, author &
former Special Assistant to the President)

Living an integrated life is a journey, not a task. There is no deadline. There is no chart or graph.

(Keith Ferrin, Founder & President,
True Success Coaching)

Where the Rubber Meets the Road

Putting the integrated life paradigm into practice is a difficult step. You may have noticed I haven't given specific solutions for your specific work situation. I haven't told you what the integrated life looks like in your job or at your office.

That's because everyone's situation is different. There is no single solution to all experiences and issues. Guided by God and his Word, through the Holy Spirit, you'll have to work out for yourself the specifics of practical integration in your situation. To help start that process, consider how each of these points might lead to greater integration in your own life:

- How should you prioritize and balance the different areas of your life?
- How can you bear the likeness of Jesus at work by exhibiting more of the fruit of the Spirit in your job?
- What are your talents and life missions, including the mission God has in mind for your work life?
- What changes in your attitude and approach to work are necessary to experience an integrated, abundant work life?
- What can you do to transform your company or marketplace?
- How can you make God your senior partner to supercharge your impact at work?

Caught in Our Own Compartments

An integrated life might seem like risky business. You might be thinking, *Why should I stick out my neck, when I could be keeping my faith below the radar screen, out of my company, and compartmentalized from my work?* Many of us would rather keep to the comfort zone of compartmentalization. But the cost of inaction is far greater than the cost of action. Quite simply, unless we integrate our faith with our work, we miss out on the abundant life God promises (John 10:10).

Since my days as an undergraduate student at Stanford University, a social psychologist named Philip Zimbardo has been legendary for powerful experiments focusing on understanding the human condition and the effects of the systems in which people operate. One of Professor Zimbardo's experiments, as I remember, involved a dog. It was brilliant, but I'm afraid it wouldn't pass political muster in our age. Dr. Zimbardo placed a young puppy in a cage, which he kept on his back porch. The cage was large enough for the dog to develop properly. The puppy was fed and cared for, and its cage was cleaned. From its cage, it could see the outside world, but it was never released to enjoy its surroundings.

The dog was fully grown after a year when Zimbardo removed the cage. The professor wanted to know how the grown dog would react to its newfound freedom. The result was startling. The dog got up and stretched from time to time, but it generally acted just as it did in the cage! Day and night, it never left its place on the porch. Though the bars of the cage were physically removed, the mental bars were still there.

Lord Byron's poem "The Prisoner of Chillon" is about a political prisoner at a castle on Lake Geneva, not far from Lausanne, Switzerland. As the story goes, the prisoner lived the better part of his life in the dungeon. Within the limits of his captivity, he made friends with spiders, mice, and rats that frequented his living space. From his cell he could see the beautiful lake and the majestic Alps that surround the castle. Finally, after many years behind bars, he was released into the wonderful world he had only seen at a distance. But the former prisoner couldn't handle the uncertainty and unfamiliarity of his new surroundings and promptly returned to the place of his captivity. He retreated to the dungeon to be with the friends he knew, the spiders, the mice, and the rats. He was more comfortable there.

These are two really sad stories. From our perspective, it's obvious both the dog and the released prisoner suffered as a result of their mental captivity. We know they didn't experience life as fully as they could have. They saw the outside, the glory of it, but they preferred the safety of living within the boundaries or compartments of their previous existence. Many of us are likewise accustomed and conditioned to living within the compartments of our own making.

Stepping Out

Each of us may privately harbor a dream. We may sense what God is calling us to, but we cannot imagine life beyond the limitations we have set for ourselves. We allow these limitations to define us. They form our comfort zone. In effect, they become our bars, our own personal prisons.

Fear often keeps us from making progress in new areas of our lives. We stay behind because we don't trust that God will lead us. God called the children of Israel out of miserable slavery in Egypt and promised them a land filled with milk and honey. A no-brainer, you'd think, but at the first sign of trouble the people were grumbling to return to the security of the traditions and bondage they'd experienced in Egypt!

It takes a concerted effort to escape the bars of a mental paradigm. John Ortberg, currently pastor of the church where I became a follower of Jesus, wrote a popular book with a title that sums up its simple yet profound message: *If You Want to Walk on Water, You've Got to Get Out of the Boat.* Using the well-known story of Jesus to illustrate the point, Ortberg challenges us to trust God and step out in faith. We want to see God do the miraculous, but we're unwilling to get out of the boat. We don't like to leave our self-imposed compartments. We won't exit the cage.

I imagine God's reaction to us is like the sadness we feel for Zimbardo's dog and the released prisoner. He wants to set us free to experience an abundant life. But we're often inclined to opt for safety, security, and the tradition of our compartmentalized lives. We're just not used to trusting God with our affairs.

We often fail to add God's power to our analysis. Looking at our "humble beginnings," we throw in the towel before we get started. Paul says, "I can do everything through him who gives me strength" (Phil. 4:13). If we would just consider God's strength and gifts, we'd find our negatives totally outweighed by his positives.

That's not to say stepping out into an integrated life will yield a trouble-free experience. It won't. Jesus told us we'd have trouble in this world. (That may be especially true if we stick out our necks and seek to transform people, practices, and organizations.) But immediately following, he admonishes us to take heart because he has overcome the world (John 16:33).

An integrated life includes a broad range of experiences, not all of them desired but all of them life-developing. I've had many tough challenges, and rarely did I enjoy going through them at the time. But those valley days always opened the door to experience the mountaintops that inevitably followed. Sometimes the way God delivers and blesses us is truly miraculous. The abundant life Jesus promised is not a trouble-free life, but it's one in which we're fulfilled by being true to God's calling.

One of the most powerful statements I've heard about stepping out of self-imposed limitations into God's calling was recently sent to me by Quest Aircraft CEO Paul Schaller, whose story we heard in Chapter 13:

"I can see now how God was preparing me through the experiences—the good, but especially the bad—to be at Quest. It took me a while to recognize that I should take on this job, but it's incredibly satisfying to wake up every day to go to work knowing that I'm close to the center of God's will for how I'll spend my life on earth. That's not to say that I don't generate enough of my own problems or that Quest doesn't face difficult challenges. He has many of us here not only as a blessing to utilize our past experiences but also as a way to

lead (minister to) others, to be 'iron sharpening iron' with each other, to have our challenges motivate us, to support and encourage each other, and to push us to reach new levels of performance.

"It's especially wonderful to know that the reason for reaching new levels is to accelerate the Word getting to remote regions of the world and helping people help those who can't help themselves and love them in the process. We find ourselves incredibly challenged to the point of closing staff meetings on our knees in prayer for a purpose that fulfills both the Great Commission 'go and make disciples of all nations, baptizing them in the name of the Father and of the Son and of the Holy Spirit, and teaching them to obey everything I have commanded you' (Matt. 28:19–20) and the Great Command 'love the Lord your God with all your heart and with all your soul and with all your mind ...love your neighbor as yourself.' (Matt. 22:37–38). I'd say that's living the abundant life, and I'm pretty blessed to be doing what I am."

Dare to Dream God's Dreams for You

When God made a covenant with Abraham, he asked him to step out and leave his tent. "Look up at the heavens and count the stars," God declared. "So shall your offspring be" (Gen. 15:5). Abraham grasped the vision and recognized God's power. He believed the promise God had for him—but only because he obeyed God and stepped out of his tent.

In his book *The Fourth Dimension*, Dr. Yonggi Cho points out that God meets us in a dimension beyond the senses of our otherwise three-dimensional lives. Some call it a sixth sense. Whatever you call it, it is God speaking to you. It's that same voice I heard those years ago, and it's the voice we hear calling us on to do what he has in mind for us.

The imperative, of course, is to embrace and follow the leading. Abraham heard God's voice, but to get a better understanding and to visualize what God had in mind, he had to get out of his tent. Has God given you an inkling of what he has in mind? Do you find yourself dreaming about what you might otherwise have or could otherwise do in your life? Many end up suffering a midlife crisis. I am convinced these midlife crises are an indication of knowing we have not done all God has called us to do. It's never too late.

What is your dream? Because it has to do with one's career, the temptation is to hesitate because it's too carnal a thought. But I hope you realize by now that your career is a part of what God has called you to. Perhaps you've written it off as inappropriate to God's plan for your life. I encourage you to go back, dust off that thought, and present your dream to God. Get out of your tent. Get out where you and God can talk about it. Put it before him, and ask him to show you what he wants you to do with it.

Years ago, my middle son, Kary, felt God was calling him to make an impact in France and Spain. The idea was in the back of his head as he attempted to follow the Lord in his work. He was led to go to business school in Spain. As he has sought God, doors have opened up to him. He's been involved in a church that started small but is now growing rapidly, as God is blessing the church. And he's been working on a business idea in Spain that the Lord brought to him. All the pieces seem to be coming together, as he is pursuing the very thing he felt God has called him to.

Taking the First Step

Each of us may privately harbor a dream. We may sense what God is calling us to, but we cannot imagine life beyond the limitations we have set for ourselves. We allow these limitations to define us. They form our comfort zone. In effect, they become our bars, our own personal prisons. Without a dream we will never take the first step.

When I attend a conference, I tend to take lots of notes. If I'm going to invest the time in a conference, something has to come out of it. So I commit to making one change as a result of the conference. The copious notes often sit in my drawer, untouched and unimplemented. But the one take-away action item I write down for Monday actually gets done. Often, that one thing makes all the difference in the world—and certainly makes the time investment worthwhile.

Start venturing into the integrated business life by taking small steps of faith where you work. Ask God to show you what specific thing you can do today to make a difference. Consider pursuing or implementing one of the ideas in the book that you may have underlined or annotated. Or sit down with a friend or spouse. Ask him or her to read this book and start a dialog. Jesus first sent his followers out two by two. If you need further encouragement or ideas, visit this book's website (www.integrated-life.org) and read the stories others have posted about efforts to integrate their lives and transform their work and home lives.

Abundance through Integrated Living

Many of us have been languishing and lacking joy in our work life. Professional life and personal life seem to be pulling us in opposite directions, and we're caught in the middle. We can't seem to get our heads above water, let alone find the time for "ministry" and our families. And we're left in a constant state of overextended burnout.

Jesus came to give us an abundance of life, a new vitality, a richer and fuller existence. Our time at work isn't excluded from Jesus' promise of abundant life. We can experience the abundance of experiencing our faith and our work integrated. Both your work life and your family life will be transformed.

The key is to understand that your spiritual life can be deeply connected with your work life and everything you do, recognize how they can be integrated—and then do it! With the help of the Holy Spirit, you can leave the old paradigms behind. You can integrate your life. Walking with the Master starts with a single step.

What's waiting for us outside? When our faith and work are integrated, we will experience the peace that comes from operating the same way in all spheres of our lives. We'll experience the power that comes from living integrated rather than compartmentalized lives. We'll view our ministry as serving others to God's glory, a holy calling in the marketplace. We will find the spiritual value and purpose in our work life. We'll see people and business transformed. We will start to see God do the outrageous in our lives.

Are you ready? Write down the one thing you are going to do differently right here, right now. Then do it. You'll never regret your first step out of the cage. This isn't the end of the book; it's the beginning of your integrated life. May the Lord bless and lead you as you do.

Author's Note

"I have come that you may have life, and have it abundantly," said Jesus. If you're unsure whether you're experiencing God's abundant life, I invite you to make a life-changing decision to follow Jesus. A personal relationship with him is the necessary first step toward an integrated life. The following is a suggested prayer:

"Lord Jesus, I need you. Thank you for dying on the cross for my sins. I open the door of my heart and receive you as my Savior and Lord. Thank you for forgiving my sins and giving me eternal life. Take control of the throne of my life. Make me the kind of person you want me to be. Teach me and help me to live an integrated life. Show me the plans you have for me. Amen."

Perhaps you just prayed this prayer to become a follower of Jesus and now want to embark on the exciting journey of integrating your newfound faith with your work. Perhaps you've been following Jesus for some time but haven't been experiencing integration in your life. In either case, please visit the book's website (www.integrated-life.org). I have assembled some resources to help get you started down the road.

When you step out to the integrated life, I guarantee you'll feel more alive, and you'll be astonished by God's grace and goodness to you through the amazing miracles he will do. Then you will have your own stories to share. I encourage you to blog about them on the website, explaining what you've tried and what God has done. Be sure to include the good and the bad. Write about how God has met you in unexpected ways. My story is not unique, and it's not the result of something special about me; it's all about God and his faithfulness.

I can't wait to read your stories.

Blessings,

Ken Eldred

Acknowledgements

Several years ago, I authored *God Is at Work*, a book on "kingdom business," or business as missions in developing nations. *The Integrated Life* is about work as ministry and is in many ways the prequel that should have been published before that book. Before we use our business experience to advance God's kingdom abroad, we must learn to advance the kingdom in our current work situations.

When I committed my life to the Lord in 1973, I realized intuitively that my life should reflect the Lord in everything that I do. I knew that meant not just in my family life but in my business life and in all other activities as well. The question was how to live such a life. Where were the examples to lead me? I realized that I was not learning how to apply my faith to many areas of my life, including my work. And I found little support in the usual places one would turn to for help.

Through years of learning by experience, help from those who encountered the same difficulties, and careful study of Scripture, I was able to understand how to apply the Word of God in the areas of my life that are not often considered areas of "biblical influence." I would like to thank those who provided guidance along that journey. I must also acknowledge those who sharpened my thinking and provided indispensable help and encouragement while I wrote this book. Unfortunately, the limited space below makes it impossible to recognize every contribution.

I would like to thank my wife, Roberta, for her encouragement to pursue the preparation of this book, even while I was engaged in many other activities. She is a constant encourager and wonderful partner. Our marriage has been a great experience. Her understanding of the Word of God and her willingness to listen and question have been invaluable. My children and their wives have also been helpful to me and have added in many ways, contributing ideas and thoughts as a result of numerous questions and varied inputs.

This book would not have been completed without the considerable efforts of Alex Brubaker, my consultant and support in preparation of much of the book. In an effort to make it easier to read and understand, we have worked, reworked, and polished the text and have reconfigured the organization of this book at least three times. We have also attempted to answer questions that might arise and augment the presentation with necessary research. I owe Alex a debt of gratitude.

My business partner, Dr. Paul Kim, has been quite helpful to me in thinking through various concepts in this book. He is prone to write pieces of Scripture on business cards and pass them out to friends. I have received a number of these over the years and find them great verses on which to meditate.

More than a dozen others helped us by reviewing the manuscript, providing helpful feedback, and raising questions, which led us to deepen the explanations of some points in the book. The list of thoughtful reviewers includes Mark Bucko, Joey Burns, Boda Chen, Justin Forman, Randy Haykin, Carl Hekkert, Brett Johnson, Brad Jung, Duane

Moyer, Richard Rock, Ben Shih, Rick Thrasher, Lisa Wagner, Jordan Winder, and Brad Zielinski. I would like to extend my deep gratitude to them and any I've missed.

Regardless of all the aid, I am still responsible for all that is written in the book. It was my call. While I have kept this effort in prayer, I am human. It's possible there are errors in fact and in my application of Scripture. My son Justin says, "When you eat a chicken, you spit out the bones." In the case you run into one of the "bones," just spit it out.

APPENDIX

A. That's What Christians Do Now

Dr. Donald E. Wildmon
President, American Family Association
December 11, 2000

In 1973 The Supreme Court said it was ok to kill unborn babies. Since then, we have killed more than the entire population of Canada. And it continues. A woman's choice? Half of those who have died in their mothers' wombs have been women. They didn't have a choice. It is called abortion.

Me? I go to church, the minister preaches, I go home. That's what Christians do now.

First, it was in dingy, dirty theaters. Then, convenience stores. Then, grocery stores. Then on television. Now it is in the homes of millions via the Internet. It is called pornography.

Me, I go to church, the minister preaches, I go home. That's what Christians do now.

They call it no-fault. Why should we blame anyone when something so tragic happens? Haven't they already suffered enough? Half of the marriages in America end this way. The children suffered.

The family broke down. It is called divorce.

Me, I go to church, the minister preaches, I go home. That's what Christians do now.

At one time it was a perversion. We kept it secret. We secured help and hope for those who practiced it. Now it is praised. We have parades celebrating it, and elected officials give it their blessing. Now it is endowed with special privileges and protected by special laws. Even some Christian leaders and denominations praise it. It is called homosexuality.

Me? I go to church, the minister preaches, I go home. That's what Christians do now.

It used to be an embarrassment. A shame. Now a third of all births are to mothers who aren't married. Two-thirds of all African-American children are born into a home without a father. The state usually pays the tab. That is why we pay our taxes, so that government can take the place of parents. After all, government bureaucrats know much better how to raise children than parents do.

It is called illegitimacy.

Me? I go to church, the minister preaches, I go home. That's what Christians do now.

At one time it was wrong. But then the state decided to legalize it, promote it and tax it. It has ripped apart families and destroyed lives. But just look at all the money the state has raised. No longer do we have to teach our children to study and work hard. Now we teach them they can get something for nothing. We spend millions encouraging people to join the fun and excitement. Just look at the big sums that people are winning. They will never have to work again!

It is called gambling.

Me? I go to church, the minister preaches, I go home. That's what Christians do now.

Not long ago, Christians were the good guys. But now any positive image of Christians in movies or on TV is gone. We are now depicted as the bad guys—greedy, narrow-minded hypocrites. The teacher can't have a Bible on her desk, but can have Playboy. We don't have Christmas and Easter holidays—just winter and spring break. We can't pray in school, but can use foul language.

It's called being tolerant.

Me? I go to church, the minister preaches, I go home. That's what Christians do now.

Yes, all these things came to pass within 30 years. Where were the Christians? Why, they were in church. All these things are for someone else to deal with. Times have changed. Involvement has been replaced with apathy.

But don't blame me. I didn't do anything. I go to church, the minister preaches, I go home.

That's what Christians do now.

B. Personal Biblical Values in Business

What are the biblical values we should be exhibiting in the marketplace? There are numerous principles the Bible espouses, and application of these values is what makes business work in God's economy. Consider reviewing each one of these values in a small group. Discuss how you could employ each principle in your business life from the position in the organization where you find yourself. Here are some questions you may find helpful to guide the conversation:

- How does practicing these values benefit business in general or your organization in particular?
- In what situations might you apply these principles?
- What might be the fallout from following these values in your workplace?
- What risks are you prepared to take?
- Who might be averse to the changes you are planning, and how could you deal with them in this situation?

Personal Character Values

The Scriptures lay out a number of personal character traits that should describe the follower of Jesus. They're important biblical values we need to exhibit at work:

> **Integrity / Honesty / Truthfulness.** "You must have accurate and honest weights and measures ... For the Lord your God detests anyone ... who deals dishonestly" (Deut. 25:15–16). "Do not steal. Do not lie. Do not deceive one another" (Lev. 19:11).
>
> **Loyalty / Faithfulness.** "A faithful man will be richly blessed" (Prov. 28:20). "The eyes of the Lord range throughout the earth to strengthen those whose hearts are fully committed to him" (2 Chr. 16:9).
>
> **Trust.** "Trust in God" (John 14:1). "Commit your way to the Lord; trust in him" (Ps. 37:5).
>
> **Commitment.** "Your hearts must be fully committed to the Lord our God, to live by his decrees and obey his commands, as at this time" (1 Ki. 8:61).
>
> **Order / Cleanliness.** "Everything should be done in a fitting and orderly way" (1 Cor. 14:40).
>
> **Hope.** "Be joyful in hope" (Rom. 12:12). "Faith is being sure of what we hope for and certain of what we do not see" (Heb. 11:1).

Interpersonal Relationship Values

God has also prescribed how we should approach our fellow man. The following biblical values deal with interpersonal relationships. They not only represent God's commands, but they represent indispensable wisdom for interacting in the marketplace:

Humility. "Do nothing out of selfish ambition or vain conceit, but in humility consider others better than yourselves" (Phil. 2:3).

Service. "Serve one another in love" (Gal. 5:13). "Serve wholeheartedly, as if you were serving the Lord, not men, because you know that the Lord will reward everyone for whatever good he does" (Eph. 6:7–8).

Respect / Dignity. "Show proper respect to everyone" (1 Pet. 2:17). "Now we ask you, brothers, to respect those who work hard among you" (1 Thess. 5:12).

Justice / Fairness. "Hate evil, love good; maintain justice in the courts" (Amos 5:15). "Then you will understand what is right and just and fair—every good path" (Prov. 2:9).

Grace / Compassion. "The Lord is full of compassion and mercy" (James 5:11). "Each one should use whatever gift he has received to serve others, faithfully administering God's grace in its various forms" (1 Pet. 4:10).

Forgiveness. "Be kind and compassionate to one another, forgiving each other, just as in Christ God forgave you" (Eph. 4:32).

Consideration. "Remind the people … to be peaceable and considerate" (Tit. 3:1–2).

Trust. "Select capable men from all the people—men who fear God, trustworthy men who hate dishonest gain—and appoint them as officials over thousands, hundreds, fifties, and tens" (Ex. 18:21).

Accountability. "Carry each other's burdens, and in this way you will fulfill the law of Christ" (Gal. 6:2). "Confess your sins to each other and pray for each other" (James 5:16).

Interdependence. "Just as each of us has one body with many members … so in Christ we who are many form one body, and each member belongs to all the others" (Rom. 12:4–5).

Love. "My command is this: Love each other as I have loved you" (John 15:12). "These three remain: faith, hope, and love. But the greatest of these is love" (1 Cor. 13:13).

Performance Values

The concepts of excellence and quality are receiving attention in management circles, but they're certainly not novel principles. God's Word commands us to serve others to the highest standard. We are to "go the extra mile" and work as if Christ were our boss, partner, or customer:

Service. "Serve wholeheartedly, as if you were serving the Lord, not men, because you know that the Lord will reward everyone for whatever good he does" (Eph. 6:7–8).

Excellence. "Whatever you do, work at it with all your heart" (Col. 3:23). "'Well done, my good servant!' his master replied" (Luke 19:17).

Diligence. "Lazy hands make a man poor, but diligent hands bring wealth" (Prov. 10:4).

Value. "If someone forces you to go one mile, go with him two miles" (Matt. 5:41).

Quality. "His work will be shown for what it is...the fire will test the quality of each man's work" (1 Cor. 3:13).

C. Livery Companies of the City of London

The emphasis on "religious fraternity" directly remains in the seal of The Worshipful Company of Skinners, one of the Great Twelve, which states in Latin, the religious language of the time, "Brothers in Christ." The English text only strengthens this sentiment. The livery company's website states, "The Skinners' motto is just as relevant today: 'To God Only Be All Glory.'"

Almost all of the London Livery Companies' seals retain their religious mottos. Some further examples from the original Great Twelve City Livery Companies:

"Serve and Obey" (the Haberdashers).

"Unto God Only Be Honor and Glory" (The Worshipful Company of Drapers).

"All Worship Be to God Only" (The Worshipful Company of Fishmongers).

"God Grant Grace" (The Worshipful Company of Grocers).

D. Resources for Further Exploration

The following is a short list of resources for further investigation of issues around faith and work. Please visit this book's website (www.integrated-life.org) for a more expansive and updated list.

Business as Mission Network	businessasmissionnetwork.com
The C12 Group	c12group.com
Convene	convenenow.com
Faith and Work Life	faithandworklife.org
God Is at Work	godisatwork.org
The High Calling	thehighcalling.org
Marketplace Leaders	marketplaceleaders.org
Regent Center for Entrepreneurship	regententrepreneur.com
Theology of Work Project	theologyofwork.org
WorkLife	worklife.org

Endnotes

1 Ray Kurzweil, "The Law of Accelerating Returns" (http://www.kurzweilai.net/meme/frame.html?main=/articles/art0134.html), accessed June 7, 2006.

2 Ibid., accessed June 7, 2006.

3 "Want Fries With Outsourcing?", *International Herald Tribune* (July 19, 2004). Quoted in Thomas L. Friedman, *The World Is Flat* (New York: Farrar, Straus & Giroux, 2005), 40–42.

4 "Where are the Jobs?", *BusinessWeek* (March 22, 2004), 36–37.

5 William I. Huyett & S. Patrick Viguerie, "Extreme Competition," *The McKinsey Quarterly* (2005 Number 1), 47–57.

6 Elizabeth Strott, "Toyota takes sales crown from GM", *MSN Money* (January 21, 2009).

7 David J. Mashburn, "The Modern Myth of Work and Life: Looking out for Number One", *Ethix* (January/February 2006), 15.

8 Adapted from William Carr Peel & Walt Larimore, *Going Public with Your Faith* (Grand Rapids, MI: Zondervan, 2003), 35–41.

9 A. W. Tozer, *The Knowledge of the Holy* (HarperSanFrancisco, 1978), 15. I am indebted to David Scott, Ph.D., of Life 2.0 for this.

10 Quoted in Peel & Larimore, *Going Public with Your Faith*, 37.

11 Robert Banks, "The Fallacy of Time Management," adapted from Robert Banks, *The Tyranny of Time* (Downers Grove, IL: InterVarsity Press, 1985). Edited for grammar. http://www.christianitytoday.com/workplace/articles/fallacyof-timemanagement.html

12 Keith Ferrin in Corey Cleek, ed., *Devotional Ventures* (Ventura, CA: Regal Books, 2006), 110–113.

13 Banks, "Fallacy of Time Management,".

14 "Talkative Teen Is Downright Perfect," *Knight-Ridder Newspapers*, April 3, 1996. Quoted in James C. Dobson, Focus On the Family Newsletter, May 1996.

15 Neil Weinberg and Nathan Vardi, "Private Inequity," *Forbes*, March 13, 2006.

16 Christian History Institute, "J. C. Penney and the Business of Being Christian," *Glimpses* Bulletin Insert #178. [chi.gospelcom.net/GLIMSEF/Glimpses/glmps178.shtml, accessed December 15, 2006]

17 John D. Beckett, *Mastering Monday* (Downers Grove, IL: InterVarsity Press, 2006), 141.

18 Chuck Ripka, interview with author, August 12, 2004.

19 Ken Eldred, *God Is at Work* (Ventura, CA: Regal Books, 2005), 62.

20 John Calvin, *Institutes of the Christian Religion* (Grand Rapids, MI: Wm. B. Eerdmans Publishing Company, 1990), III.x.6.

21 Ken Shigematsu, "Justice and Mercy: Proverbs 19-17" (sermon, October 15, 2006), 10th Avenue Church, Vancouver, Canada. (http://kensmessage.blogspot.com/2006/10/justice-and-mercy-proverbs-19-17-oct15.html), accessed February 27, 2008.

22 Brian Griffiths, *Capitalism, Morality and Markets* (London: Institute of Economic Affairs, 2001), 20–25.

23 Catherine Williams, "Sarbanes-Oxley Deadline Reopens Floodgates for Service Firms," *Mass High Tech: The Journal of New England Technology*, June 16, 2006 (http://www.bizjournals.com/masshightech/stories/2006/06/19/story1.html), accessed June 26, 2006.

24 Amitai Etzioni, "When It Comes to Ethics, B-Schools Get an F", *Washington Post*, August 4, 2002, B04.

25 Charles Duhigg, "Ethicists At the Gate", *The Harbus*, January 14, 2003.

26 Etzioni, "When It Comes to Ethics", B04.

27 Ibid.

28 Brian Griffiths, *Capitalism, Morality and Markets* (London: Institute of Economic Affairs, 2001), 35.

29 JCPenney.net, "On the Golden Rule and Its Application in Business" www.jcpenney.net/company/history/history/archive15.htm, accessed December 15, 2006.

30 John Woodbridge, ed., *More Than Conquerors* (Chicago: Moody Press, 1992), 340.

31 Eldred, *God Is at Work*, 97–98.

32 Theodore Roosevelt Malloch, *Social, Human and Spiritual Capital in Economic Development*, metanexus.net, April 19, 2006.

33 Max Weber, *The Protestant Ethic and the Spirit of Capitalism* (London: Routledge Classics, 2002).

34 Stephen Haber, Douglass C. North, & Barry R. Weingast, "If Economists Are So Smart, Why Is Africa So Poor?" *Wall Street Journal*, July 30, 2003.

35 *Where is the Wealth of Nations?: Measuring Capital for the 21st Century* (Washington DC: The World Bank, 2006), 4, 162.

36 Ibid., 4, 92-96.

37 Theodore Roosevelt Malloch, *Spiritual Enterprise* (forthcoming manuscript), Chapter 1.

38 Dennis M. Mahoney, "A Growing Flock," *The Columbus Dispatch* (January 31, 2003).

39 Eldred, *God Is at Work*, 91–93.

40 Quoted in Laura Nash, *Believers in Business* (Nashville, Tennessee: Thomas Nelson, 1994), 230.

41 Peter Drucker, *The Essential Drucker* (New York: HarperCollins, 2001).

42 "R. G. LeTourneau: No Job Too Big," In Sight Ministries (http://www.intouch.org/site/c.dhKHIXPKIuE/b.2704871/k.EDBE/Life_Principles_Center__Life_Examples__R_G_LeTourneau.htm), accessed August 16, 2007.

43 Dallas Willard, *The Spirit of the Disciplines* (San Francisco: HarperSanFrancisco, 1999), 213.

44 John Stott, *Issues Facing Christians Today* (Basingstoke, U.K.: Marshalls, 1984), 162. Quoted in Joyce Avedisian, "Spirituality of Work: An Investigation," an InterVarsity Ministry in Daily Life Reflection at http://www.ivmdl.org/reflections.cfm?study=69.

45 Doug Sherman & William Hendricks, *Your Work Matters to God* (Colorado Springs, CO: NavPress, 1987), 77-80.

46 Ibid., 101–103.

47 Ibid., 84.

48 R. Paul Stevens, *The Other Six Days: Vocation, Work, and Ministry in Biblical Perspective* (Grand Rapids, MI: Wm. B. Eerdmans Publishing Company, 2000), 81–82.

49 Quoted by Gordon Preece, "Work" in Robert Banks and R. Paul Stevens, *The Complete Book of Everyday Christianity* (Downers Grove, IL: InterVarsity Press, 1997), 1126.

50 Dorothy L. Sayers, *Creed or Chaos?* (Manchester, NH: Sophia Institute Press, 1995).

51 Alistair Mackenzie & Wayne Kirkland, *Where's God on Monday?* (Colorado Springs, CO: NavPress, 2003), 84.

52 Eldred, *God Is at Work*, 304–305. I am indebted to Dave Evans, co-founder of Electronic Arts, as the source for this framework.

53 Richard C. Chewning, John W. Eby, & Shirley J. Roels, *Business Through the Eyes of Faith* (San Francisco: HarperSanFrancisco, 1990), 4.

54 The phrase "repurposing business" is ® of The Institute.

55 Sayers, *Creed or Chaos?*, 77. Quoted in Peel & Larimore, *Going Public with Your Faith*, 37.

56 Sherman & Hendricks, *Your Work Matters to God*, 16.

57 WorkLife website (http://www.hischurchatwork.org/partner/Article_Display_Page/0,,PTID61609 | CHID175864 | CIID1800670,00.html), accessed August 23, 2006.

58 A. W. Tozer, *The Pursuit of God* (Harrisburg, PA: Christian Publications, Inc., 1948), Ch. 10. Quoted in John D. Beckett, *Loving Monday* (Downers Grove, IL: InterVarsity Press, 1998), 71.

59 Beckett, *Loving Monday*, 67.
60 Tozer, *Pursuit of God*, Ch. 10. Quoted in Beckett, *Loving Monday*, 71.
61 Dallas Willard, *The Spirit of the Disciplines* (San Francisco: HarperSanFrancisco, 1999), 214.
62 Sayers, *Creed or Chaos?*, 76–77. Quoted in Peel & Larimore, *Going Public with Your Faith*, 35.
63 Ray Bystrom, "Ten Words for Those Who Work: Church," *The Marketplace* (bi-monthly publication of Mennonite Economic Development Associates), January/February 1995.
64 While local church bodies often engage in worship corporately as well, worship is for our own personal encouragement, edification, development, and relationship with God. It is quite frankly the key pillar on which the church, God's people, rests. Activity without personal worship is just that—activity.
65 Bystrom, "Ten Words for Those Who Work: Church."
66 Bob Smith, *When All Else Fails ... Read the Directions* (Waco, Texas: Word Books,
1974), 62.
67 Phone interview with Charlie Paparelli. "Worklife Momentum" (newsletter of WorkLife), April 2007.
68 David Loveless bio (http://www.willowcreek.com/aoe/Session3-loveless-bio.asp), accessed October 31, 2007.
69 Phone interviews with Jim Butler and David Loveless, October 31 and November 7, 2007.
70 Durwood Snead, "Business Is Sacred at North Point" (http://www.businessasmissionnetwork.com/2007/09/business-is-sacred-at-north-point.html), accessed September 19, 2007.
71 Os Guinness, "Belief or Unbelief," *Today God Is First* newsletter, December 5, 2006.
72 Howard Gardner, *Frames of Mind: The Theory of Multiple Intelligences* (New York: Basic Books, 1983).
73 Thomas Sowell, "Random Thoughts," August 29, 2006. [www.townhall.com/columnists/ThomasSowell/2006/08/29/random_thoughts; accessed January 14, 2007]
74 John Stott, *Involvement*, vol. 2 (Old Tappan, NJ: Flaming H. Revell, 1985), 30.

75 Alistair Mackenzie & Wayne Kirkland, *Where's God on Monday?* (Colorado Springs, CO: NavPress, 2003), 30.

76 Ken Blanchard & Barbara Glanz, *The Simple Truths of Service* (Simple Truths, 2005), 12–39.

77 Personal interview with Paul Schaller.

78 Eldred, *God Is at Work*, 239–241, 245–246.

Other Books
By Ken Eldred

God Is at Work:
Transforming People
and Nations Through
Business

Ken Eldred

Named the number one
book in the field by the
Business as Mission
Network!

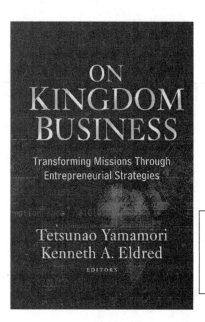

*On Kingdom Business:
Transforming
Missions Through
Entrepreneurial
Strategies*

Ken Eldred & Ted
Yamamori, Eds.

**Winner of a
2004 Christianity Today
Book Award!**